TOTAL FEARS

Total

Letters to Dubenka

Fears

Bohumil Hrabal

Translated from the Czech by James Naughton

TWISTED SPOON PRESS • PRAGUE

ISBN 80-902171-9-2

CONTENTS

The Magic Flute

Sometimes when I get up and emerge from the mists of slumber, my whole room hurts, my whole bedroom, the view from the window hurts, kids go to school, people go shopping, everybody knows where to go, only I don't know where I want to go, I get dressed, blearily, stumbling, hopping about to pull on my trousers, I go and shave with my electric razor — for years now, whenever I shave, I've avoided looking at myself in the mirror, I shave in the dark or round the corner, sitting on a chair in the passage, with the socket in the bathroom, I don't like looking at myself any more, I'm scared by my own face in the bathroom, I'm hurt even by my own appearance, I see yesterday's drunkenness in my eyes, I don't even have breakfast any more, or if I do, only coffee and a cigarette, I sit at the table, sometimes my hands give way under me and several times I repeat to myself, Hrabal, Hrabal, Bohumil Hrabal, you've victoried yourself away, you've reached the peak of emptiness, as my Lao Tzu taught me, I've reached the peak of emptiness and everything hurts, even the walk to the bus-stop hurts, and the whole bus hurts as well, I lower my guilty-looking eyes, I'm afraid of looking people in the eye, sometimes I cross my palms and extend my wrists, I hold out my hands so that people can arrest me and hand me over to the cops, because I feel guilty even about this once too loud a solitude which isn't loud any longer, because I'm hurt not only by the escalator which takes me down to the infernal regions below, I'm hurt even by the looks of the people travelling up, each of them has somewhere to go, while I've reached the peak of emptiness and don't know where I want to go. I know, but in the end I'm saved by those children of mine, the little cats in the woods, who are waiting for me, they're my children, so I take the metro, but now even the metro hurts, people go up, while others, and I with them, go down, we stand in our places, going down the escalator, then up the stairs I go again, and there in the little buffet I guiltily buy four grilled chicken breasts, and guiltily I pay, watching my hands tremble, because I'm buying chicken for the cats, while out there somewhere in Africa children starve. Even that little buffet hurts, and the busy street, with its trucks and private cars criss-crossing in opposite directions, every driver knows where to go, I'm the only one who doesn't, even if out there somewhere in the woods my last hopes are there waiting for me, the last reason to live, my little cats, petrified, in case I never come, what would become of them, who would feed them, who would stroke them, because they love me, those kitties, whereas I'm hurt now, not just by my own little bedroom, I'm hurt by this whole town in which I live, I'm hurt by this whole world, because towards morning certain beings come to me — beings not unfamiliar to me, on the contrary, they come slowly but surely up the escalator of my soul, and not only their faces come into focus, but also certain horrible events, just like a portrait, or a film, a documentary not only about how I was ever madly in love, but also how I failed people. So that interior monologue continues, no, I'm no longer talking alone with myself, but it's as if I'm up before an interrogating judge, everything I ever said, everything I ever did, everything is always against me, from this time on whatever I've been made to think about has been against me. How many times I've crossed the road at the red, how many times I've walked through the stream of traffic, but in spite of being lost in thought, I am accompanied always by my guardian angel, my little guardian angel, because this guardian angel of mine wants me to remain in this world as yet, in order to reach the final bottom, to go down yet one more flight, to the place of the ultimate pit of remorse, because the whole world hurts, and even that guardian angel of mine hurts, how many times I've felt like jumping from the fifth floor, from my apartment where every room hurts, but always at the last moment my guardian angel saves me, he pulls me back, just like my Herr Doktor Franz Kafka, who wanted to jump from the fifth floor, from the Maison Oppelt, which you enter from the Old Town Square, but the Herr Doctor would have fallen into Pařížská, into Paris Avenue, he too was hurt by the world, I suppose, and hurt by his life, just like Malte Laurids Brigge, who also wanted to jump from the fifth floor, he was hurt too by the world in Paris. Brigge was hurt by the whole world as well, just like Rainer Maria Rilke.

I've victoried myself away, I've reached the peak of emptiness. Now I have what I've cooked up for myself, it's here. The poet Konstantin Biebl jumped out of the window, but first, and this was a long time before, he had Štyrský paint him a picture, of a man falling backwards out of a window, just like turning the page of a book. So. And Arthur Schopenhauer's dad also committed suicide. And Seneca in Salamanca too. But I'm not going to jump out of any window, it's not that my guardian angel's talked me out of it, but he's whispered, that he who bestowed upon me this peak of emptiness has told him it just wouldn't do to go out as easily as that, I have to re-experience that feeling of the whole world hurting, like the last Chinese emperor, whom they didn't execute, they just rinsed his brains out for twelve years to make him know all that he'd done, to make him reach, not the peak of emptiness, but the state of being an ordinary person, who goes out shopping just like anyone else, to make him human. So every day I ride on the bus, that's my travelling confessional, I travel once into town and back again the same day, like trams and trains and aeroplanes, once there and once back again . . .

So I sit in the bus, chewing on a roll, then take another, sweeping the crumbs from my lap and thinking, thinking of the pub, where the drunkards give me their fragments of sentences, as if it was all they lived for, to save up these morsels specially to please me, or wound me . . . they know very well I carry a little notebook with me everywhere in my head . . . when I ask, how's life? — it's as if they've already rehearsed this poem of theirs, their life's credo . . . Life? Morning suicidal, work till midday, lunch at the canteen, afternoon I do more of the same old slog, then I'm back to the Myrtle, the Green Laboratory, I knock back one beer after another, non-stop, till the last one, and so on into the evening . . . Christmas Eve . . . morning suicidal . . . and so on . . . why is he telling me this, this drunkard of mine, who's just waiting for me, so as to tell me . . . Today I feel like I survived an air-raid that never happened . . . and another time . . . Instead of my head I can feel this pressure-cooker . . . Bóžo, Bohouušku, Božku . . . he says, to make me hear him out and remember what he said, for ever . . . and there he sits, arms folded, always in his overcoat, sitting there like a wounded dove . . . and yes, I remember, when a dead pigeon lies on the asphalt, always, before maybe finally getting squashed by a car tyre, it would lie there, so lovely in death, as if arranged for my viewing, like that poem by Nezval, 'The Drowned Woman in the Seine' . . .

And then I sit here in my travelling confessional, and I'm made to finish imagining these images which visit me, which I heard people tell, and now, all at once, it's making that room of mine where I sleep hurt even more, making the whole world hurt . . . Somewhere over in Germany, in a town beside a lake, every evening a blazing swan would fly up into the air, and after it had finished burning, it would fall down into the surface of the lake, the locals were horrified, so they organised some patrols and they caught a young man, who had just lured another swan with a bread roll, he poured a bottle of petrol over it, and lit it, delighting himself with the sight of this blazing swan soaring up into the night . . . and when they caught him, he was a young man, who said in his defence, that he was inspired by Salvador Dali, a painting of a burning giraffe had disturbed him so much at night that it made the room hurt, where he dreamt about this blazing giraffe and Salvador Dali's paranoiac-critical method, he'd wanted to pour petrol over a giraffe at the zoo to see its mane catch fire, but he couldn't reach up that high, so he'd lured over a trusting swan, and when it soared up blazing into the sky, he saw it rise to the zenith before it fell, he saw Salvador Dali's burning giraffe . . . and the world stopped hurting, and he didn't know how that image would strike me, like the surface of the pond which the once lovely swan hit in its cooling descent . . .

So I sit in the bus, I know the road off by heart, so that even if I close my eyes, I know, I feel with my body, from the feel of the asphalt and the road paving I know where I am, the bus-driver's gear-changes make me sense which corner we are at, the impacts of the brake tell me what hazards are encountered on the road . . . So even that little room in my head hurts, I heard the story about the swan, but the stuff about the burning giraffe and the paranoiac-critical method is something I didn't just wilfully append, it's the way my mind works, it comes leaping in, what I hear is insufficient, it's not good enough, I have to make up the rest, because that's part and parcel of my trade, something not chosen by me, but forced upon me, something which once I delighted in, while I was strong, and thus could take pleasure in what I was honoured by, this serious game, which now horrifies me, just as once I used to be proud of being a drinker, even though I didn't like the stuff, of being a young hooligan, like the poet Yesenin, and I didn't make up the bit about him dying young, whereas I shall soon be seventy-five . . . so now I'm alone against myself, because I've just victoried myself away, when I reached that loud solitude . . . that emptiness, which mirrors and resonates all the pains of the world, even though I bewitch myself often with Yesenin's verses . . . "Home shall I go again, delight in others' happy health, then in the green dusk beneath the window go and hang myself . . ."

The Gods have deserted this land, the heroes of antiquity have departed, Hercules and Prometheus . . . My wife found it better to depart this life also, just like Pearl, daughter of the rabbi from Bratislava, she who loved me and I her, because she was so much like my wife Pipsi, this Sunday I experienced dusk with a blood-red sun setting over Prague and cinnamon clouds before sunset prophesying a gale, the Old Town Square was blocked off by huge yellow vehicles with grid fencing and a PUBLIC SECURITY sign, and on Kaprová water cannon were gushing, sweeping pedestrians under cars, people were recovering in an alcove from being beaten a moment before, an elbow crutch and an eighty-year-old lady crying out: Who's going to pay for soaking my precious fur-coat? A group of militia men stood in front of Umprum, the Academy of Applied Arts, demanding access, the windows of Umprum were lit up, with the figures of art-students flitting to and fro, twice a year they have a two-day celebration of the end of term, once now halfway through the year, and again at the end of the year . . . A young man came with a key, the militia men demanded he unlock the door for them, but the young man, the lecturer, said, This is academic ground, you're not allowed in, but one of them said he would have to let all of them in, because a moment ago three men had entered the building in masked hoods with only peepholes for the eyes, but the young assistant said he would inspect the place himself and tell them the result of his investigation, he went inside and locked the door behind him . . . Meanwhile in the subways to the metro people were weeping, not with emotion, but with teargas, the police on the streets were arresting people who were soaked to the skin — I didn't go to the Myrtle, because there was a sign saying it was closed "for technical reasons", so I went to U Ottů, and a young man in a green sweater sat down at one of the neighbouring tables, then three more came and sat themselves down behind me and our table, and they were dressed in anoraks and coloured sweaters too, these young policemen on duty, they looked like footballers, we looked each other up and down, and I was fearful, gazing with unblinking eyes into the very heart of quietude and silence, because the gods had left this world and this city, that Sunday evening I reached that true loud solitude and summit of emptiness, I reached that final perturbation attained by Kierkegaard and Friedrich Nietzsche. So many times I had wanted to jump from the window on the fifth floor where I live, not because of this, but because of watching my Pipsi dying all that long time, my wife, whom Pearl resembled so closely, but when I read that Kafka had wanted to jump from the fifth floor of the house where he lived, the Maison Oppelt, a wholesale wine merchant's with up to seven hundred thousand bottles of valuable wines stored under the Old Town Square, when I read that Malte Laurids Brigge also lived in Paris on the fifth floor, when I learnt about those various fifth floors, I postponed my jump out of the window — and if I had the strength, I too would buy a can of petrol and set fire to myself, but I'm afraid, I'm not brave like that, I'm not like Mucius Scaevola, that young man who burned his left hand in front of the horrified gaze of his enemies, declaring that Rome could boast a thousand others like him. I'm afraid, and in the end, I like being afraid, being full of that final perturbation, just like Kierkegaard, just like Nietzsche, I, who have eyes full of tears and am drenched, just like those who tasted the tear-gas with their own eyes, with their own bodies the streaming impact of the water cannon, thanks to my imagination and my own tactile experience, which others felt both body and soul . . .

This Sunday, however, I understood why twenty years ago, when readers gave me copies of my books for signature, I inscribed them with one of two localities — "At the Golden Tiger" or "In Gallicien" — already twenty years back I noticed how people were starting to get those shifted eyes, like the sons of the Rabbi of Belz and Jews in general used to have . . .

Coming into Prague from Kersko on Monday, I got out at the Museum at a quarter past three, and I saw the statue of Saint Wenceslas towering menacingly in its full armour, around it, with their backs to the royal steed, policemen were walking — young men with their uniform coats drawn back into a great tuck at the rear, to make their chests more prominent, I saw streams of people passing around those who stood on the kerb gazing at the spot where those who, not explicitly forbidden, but also not allowed, wished to lay their bouquet of flowers, from the pavement opposite there came the sound of whistles on fingers, and I saw more of the same sort of policemen standing on pavements and kerbs as those who were offering Saint Wenceslas unwanted protection and aid, I saw a policeman leading a whistler off through the crowd and into a passage . . . but this time I didn't need tear-gas any more, I wept silently about how the gods seemed really to have abandoned this world, Hercules was gone, Prometheus was also gone, those forces which made the world turn were gone, and all that remained was not the burning bush, but the burning young student, Jan Palach, who in that moment of burning "was what he was". If I'd been there with him at that moment, I'd have asked him on bended knee to burn indeed, but differently, to burn with the word which might become flesh, which might help those who were not yet burning, or if they were, then burning with spirit and in spirit. But it happened as it did. O my Father, if it be possible, let this cup pass from me . . . Christ also did not wish to be nailed on the cross. But in the end it happened as it happened, just as in Prague a match, such as you'd use to light a child's firework or a cigarette, a match kindled all that was mortal in a man, and left behind only a memory, which still fires those who protest today against the presence of foreign armies in the land. And so I walked along with my head bowed, and suddenly I realised I'd met girls' hands coming up, holding fragile bunches of montbretia and carnations gently in their fingers, so as not to harm them. And over the bunches of flowers I saw these young women's eyes, wide open as if they were going to communion or a Bach mass, I went back with one of them, she paused a while on the pavement near Saint Wenceslas, then, followed by all the eyes of the onlookers she crossed the road, she hesitated a moment, she stopped even, but then with a gentle move of the hand a young policeman took her across to the other pavement. By now it was half past three, down by the Koruna snack bar a group of punks were sitting, an equally young policeman was leafing with trembling fingers through one of their ID cards, they were punks, their cases of musical instruments were there on the centre island, but smiles and calm shone from their eyes, and I was ashamed that I had reached this peak of emptiness and loud solitude, had reached a "final state of perturbation" and was no longer good for anything — if I received some prize or other, some award for literature, if I had any character, I'd at least burn that piece of paper attesting to who I am not — because if I was in fact the man I think I am and my readers think I am, I'd have taken that trembling bunch of flowers tenderly out of that girl's hand and placed it beneath the hoof of Saint Wenceslas's horse . . . but I know I've no longer got it in me, by mistake I'd get what was coming to me, as the water cannon broke my back and the sharp needle of that tear-gas tore out my eyes, like Oedipus Rex, crushed by fate, tearing his eyes out of their sockets . . .

But how cheap and easy it is, Mister Hrabal, to say, like Heidegger, that the gods have abandoned this world, that Hercules is gone, and Prometheus, it's fine to listen to all this, Mister Hrabal, but the contents of such sentences are a few pennyworth for a hundred grams of cheap brawn, because one young student of philosophy, Mister Heidegger, demonstrated that maybe the old gods have died, but new gods are born, who have to pay the price, even if it's only the severed ear of Vincent van Gogh, who needed no myths, yet whose works made this visible world transparent . . .

So what has really happened here in this city over the last two days? I reckon it was the armed forces of the police and militia grossly interfering in the affairs of young people who had created their own myth of a saint, I reckon it was the armed forces assuming the right to overstep the bounds of necessary defence against people who used neither firearms, stones, nor sticks, who brought only their words and two-fingered whistles, who even brought along a child in a pram — but it wasn't even like when Ulysses was ploughing, and they placed his little son in the furrow, so that the mighty might compel him to fight in the Trojan War . . . Still, what of it? Eyes will be rinsed with tears, and Ophtal is stronger than tear-gas, clothes will dry out or new ones can be bought, and detained youths will eventually be released. Life will rattle back on to its old tracks . . . Really, Mister Hrabal? On to its old tracks? No way! Those young people who participated actively, or even in spirit, in mind, represent a certain commitment, a certain act of solidarity and positive homage to a certain Good, which must be redeemable sometime in the future . . .

So I sat in the Golden Tiger and I thought, as I'm always doing, about how, if the gods really loved me, I would just drop dead over a glass of beer, I sat and attended to the details of that great Monday and great Sunday, and those tidings recited by flaming eyes rolled themselves out for me into a great carpet, which cannot be rescinded or burnt, because its contents occurred, they were sewn and stitched by reality, and what has happened cannot be undone. There in the Golden Tiger I dreamt of my own death, drinking my couple of beers, today I had six, and everything I heard and paid attention to, everything came off its hinges, it turned into a buzz of human conversation which stopped making any sense, so I paid, and after they'd given me a free beer, I went out into the night — I lifted my head, and as always I gazed up at the sky, the sky above the church of St. Giles, it'll be a cold starry night, diagonally out of my window on the fifth floor I'll be able to see the sickle moon — I went off, and Pařížská was quiet now, a police van went past, it stopped quietly, the officer got out and quietly placed a summons behind the wipers of the cars parked where parking isn't allowed, and then the headlamps moved quietly on to the Maison Oppelt, where Franz Kafka once wanted to jump from the fifth floor, and then I stood alone in the Old Town Square, nobody else was there, I sat myself down on the nearest bench and began to dream . . . Opposite me rose the monument to Master Jan Hus — when Jan Hus was being burnt at the stake, one old lady brought him a little bit more brushwood, to make him burn better — the monument was there in darkness in the middle of the square, while the Kinsky Palace, its walls and the whole eastern wall of the square were shining, lit up by the bright sodium lamps, so that the black silhouette of the memorial stood out against the pink and beige walls of the palaces and houses — and as I sat there alone, a young man jumped up on the benches and started running along them, jumping from one bench to another, and from the heart of the Old Town Square there came the quiet sound of a flute, a soft, quiet, yet insistent sound of a flute, as if it were pouring out from some lonely secluded spot, from mountain pasture, or a solitary lake, that flute sound was moving purely in itself, but also because only a few hours ago the last vehicles with their water cannon and teargas had left this place, the last vehicles with their Alsatian dogs, those beautiful German sheepdogs, who must be back in their kennels by now, after the exertions of Sunday and Monday . . . But here on the Old Town Square the sound of the flute floated right out of the heart of the monument, it quite startled me, I stood up, raised a hand, and turned my head . . . and sure enough, the sound of that flute was rising up and spreading out all over the square from those shrubs where the statue of Master Jan Hus towers up — out of those evergreens, which never wither even in winter, the sound of that flute rose, and several pedestrians passed, their voices loud in the emptiness of the square, but nobody stopped, the footsteps criss-crossed diagonally from Železná to Pařížská, from Dlouhá to Melantrišská, and then the sound of the flute ceased, there was silence like a tensed string about to burst, and I saw, by the kerb around Jan Hus, how the fronds parted and someone jumped out on to the paving stones, which shone in the middle distance from the lit-up walls, and then I saw a second figure emerge from the black monument, holding a children's pram — out of the black darkness of the monument, and into the bright light beside what was once the pharmacy U Jednorožce, The Unicorn, there came a young woman and a young man, pushing that pram, where perhaps the magic flute now lay, but I, being a man of letters, glanced up at the first-floor window of the old pharmacy and remembered that this was the site of Berta Fanta's salon, where the conversation back in Habsburg days was joined by Franz Kafka, Albert Einstein, Rudolf Steiner, Max Brod, and by Polish poets . . . And the magic children's pram turned into the Royal Route, a taxi turned in from Pařížská, and raising my hand I stopped its lit-up diadem . . . and when I got into the taxi, I realised that the sound of the magic flute had come from that place where the monument's vertical message unfurls . . . "I believe that the rule of the people of Thy cause will return again into Thy hands . . ."

P.S.

And at home I found the ending of the third part of T. S. Eliot's *The Waste Land* and I read it to the moon from the fifth floor . . . Burning burning burning burning / O Lord Thou pluck-est me out / O Lord Thou pluckest / burning

And in the notes to it I found that this text is from the Fire Sermon . . . written by Buddha.

Kersko, Tuesday 17th January 1989

Public Suicide

Dear Dubenka,

Ever since I got back from the "Delighted States", from that journey you planned for me so preposterously and so fondly, maybe just so that we could see each other again, ever since that time I've been off the rails . . . It's like what happened to my mother, who, according to her death certificate, died of softening of the brain — but I've attained such an absolute peak of emptiness and I'm so, so alone, effectively in solitary confinement, tied up in a straitjacket, no longer living in time, but only and exclusively in space, which shocks and horrifies me . . .

One day an Italian who came to Prague by marriage, a young man who restores chapels, invited me to come out and see this thing he'd seen in Budeč — to where Saint Wenceslas would ride out to visit his grandmother Ludmila, later strangled with a scarf — and there in Budeč in the dome of the rotunda, rest the mouldered, mouldering bones of hundreds of generations of doves, who, whenever they sense their time has come, fly into the dome to die, several whole centuries of them there are, down beneath nothing but humus, guano, layer upon layer of generations of doves in that rounded dome, rising up from the pluperfect tense via the imperfect to the dove feathers and bones of the year that's just past . . .

So that's me, I who have aged so much now that I live and feed off childhood memories, these layers of mine are there somehow in the receding strata of that dove sepulchre in Budeč — all I have to do is close my eyes and I'm back there, back in Židenice, where I was born in the bed in which my grandfather later died, in a room which meant everything to me, because from the moment I opened my eyes there was always sunshine in that room, or if not sunshine, light at least . . . Our street, Balbínova, sloped up a hill, the pavement passed our pair of windows, and as people went up and down the street their heads either rose up or descended, severed by the two window-frames . . . That is my light, the little house on Balbínova, in Židenice, where my unmarried mother gave birth to me, where my granny and granddad brought me up, that street of mine with its little low houses and that sunlight . . . I've always thought of the room where I was born as a little church or a room in a chateau, with its holy pictures and the Virgin Mary under a glass cover, and huge asparagus ferns, and a plush-covered table and on it a huge plush-covered book with a gold fastening, it looked like a bible, that family album, which I was afraid to open . . . Outside the windows were fields of maize and fruit trees and the rising hillside, where a vineyard ran and grandma had a field . . . When the time came, she took me with her, she hoed the tomatoes and beans, picked the gooseberries and currants, and again when it was time, she clambered about the trees picking the various damsons, plums and apricots, while I sat staring . . . What did I stare at? Nothing, I was simply there with granny, always bathed in sunlight, even if it started to drizzle . . .

Dubenka, just like I remember those first three years of my life, living with my grandmother, so I remember you now, I see you in light, you're dressed in light, you even have a halo, because you're so far away, because, Dubenka, then it came to pass, when I was four years old, they took me away to Polná, to the brewery, where the sun never entered, I lived there with my new dad and my mother, a stranger to me, and in that brewery apartment you had to have the lamp on even during the day, for sunlight you had to go into the yard or off into town . . . So I became a runaway, who always stayed out of doors till bedtime . . . I'm no different now, Dubenka, I'm just the same — the sun only comes out when I remember you, and even if it's a rainy day . . . I can still see you that first time you came to the pub the Golden Tiger, with your rucksack on your back. I was sitting under the little antlers, at the back of the pub where they have to leave the light on, you were searching for a face to match the name, and then you came up and you introduced yourself as April Gifford, studying Czech, you expected I'd be cross at you barging in like that . . . but I knew right away, my future was in your eyes, I melted, and so did my friends, you sat down with us and had some beer, and Mr Marysko said . . . April . . .? Aprilka . . .? No, we'll call you Dubenka . . . And from then on you were Dubenka . . . for April in Czech is "duben", the "oak month" . . . And when you took off your jacket, spattered with rain, somebody inquired: Is it raining out there? And you said . . . Yes folks, Mr Hrabal, it's raining, or as you Czechs say, it's pissing down . . . Hearing that, all the customers burst out laughing and they gave you a special look, as if you'd stroked them or something . . . And when we asked you where you were from, you told us, repeating the answer several times: Ze "Spokojených" států . . . From the "Delighted" States . . . But you pleased the customers most of all when, in reply to a question from our former Consul: So what do they teach you on that Slavic course, what good things have you learnt? you said guilelessly: Well, stuff like, for example — what a smart-ass Party we have . . . Hearing this, our Consul was tickled pink, and he said . . . This girl must come again! she's a sweet child . . . So now you'd introduced yourself, Dubenka, to the Golden Tiger — and I think once again of that young archaeologist, who showed me the excavated dome of that Romanesque church, all those layers of dead doves and pigeons — through the deep probe in its side I saw several centuries back, back to where the bones and feathers had turned to nothing but guano and humus, while there up above lay the dead doves, who, before they died, decorously spread out their wings like fans and tucked up their tiny heads, just as Lady Death, the dovely reaper has contrived it . . . O Colomba, Colomba, my little dove . . . as it is written in the Ursuline Church, where tiny, lace-wrapped Colomba rests, her bones that were brought to Prague by the Father of our Nation, the Emperor Charles IV . . . the Saint who preferred to die, rather than marry the one she did not love, she sleeps her sleep along with the Ursulines, like the doves in their layers do in the dome of the Romanesque rotunda of Budeč near Prague . . .

Dear Dubenka, I'm writing to you from our metropolis, where once it was the custom for flocks of doves and pigeons to toddle about and coo in the city squares, and people took photographs of themselves with them, and gave them titbits to eat . . . Those city squares were even a kind of witness to our legendary dove-like nature . . . But it's no longer so, a while ago I started coming across men in a kind of official garb, like a zookeeper's uniform, they looked like gnomes or inmates of some institution, they even wore goggles, maybe so as not to be identified, great preternaturally huge goggles with lenses like two yoghurts. There they were, walking about in the early hours of the morning, going through the streets and squares, scattering poisoned grain or catching pigeons in nets, like the little butterfly nets we had as children. Often I would meet these monsters already bearing their prey, holding a kind of fishing net, each one full of topsy-turvy wings, helpless red feet rammed through the netting, in every net you saw one or two pairs of horrified dove's eyes, those beautiful eyes . . . And nobody stopped them, everyone was dismayed at those human monsters carting off their prey . . . hundreds of innocent dove's eyes . . . Yet every May the First, at every festival, every children's fun and games in city squares and Parks of Leisure and Culture, everywhere the blue banners fluttered and the blue flags waved in children's fingers bearing that white dove, painted for the Peace Movement by Pablo Picasso . . .

I live in a city where for at least the last two years a campaign has been waged against doves and pigeons, they're just vanishing more and more . . . here and there one struts out or a little group of them, pecking whatever people throw at them . . . but watch it, because according to the newspapers and magazines it's forbidden now, doves and pigeons are a danger to human health . . . and feeding them is undesirable, almost a punishable offence . . . I've even seen people kicking over-confiding ones out of the way, they just kick them out of the way, and there are people who shout and threaten to make an official complaint, when they see somebody feeding those beautiful, innocent pigeons — that dove-like nature of ours . . .

Everything is changing here, Dubenka, and there's no end to it, already the voices have been heard saying that swans are dangerous too, that a swan is liable to kill ducklings with its lovely black bill . . . Thousands of swans have flown into Prague to find a quiet safe haven, where they live by begging, and they in turn reward people with their elegance, they are our fashion models, our white mannequins, Prague is a fluvial Swan Lake several miles long . . . and this is also starting to bother, not just the hunting and shooting fraternity, but also people like me, because I too can see how the ducklings disappear and only the ducks remain on the Vltava . . . What's to be done about it? In England at least the swans belong to the Queen, and anybody who maims or kills a swan, is prosecuted — in England maiming or killing a swan is a crime of *lèse majesté* . . .

But, I reckon, Dubenka, happiness is always cheek by jowl with lurking misfortune. Once when I was in Moscow, as a guest of UNESCO, for celebrations of the millenium of the Russian Orthodox Church, we went to open a monastery in deep snow — it looked in that snow as if it hung in heaven itself — its walls were blue and its pillars white . . . and that heavenly chanting! Ruslan and Ludmila, a thousand years ago, after wandering all over the Mediterranean, finally witnessed Orthodox mass in Constantinople, and they were so moved by it, that they asked each other: Are we still on earth or already in heaven? And all at once they knew that for the Russians Orthodoxy would be number one . . . I was invited along with the rest to meet Patriarch Pimen, and when my turn came, I told the Patriarch that once I'd given a lecture in a crystal palace on *Zum ewigen Frieden*, the subject of a little book which Immanuel Kant wrote in nearby Kaliningrad, formerly Koenigsberg, founded by the Bohemian ruler Přemysl Otakar II . . . After I'd summarized its contents, I enquired of the Patriarch . . . Would you be so kind as to tell me — you know how in Hebrew Emanuel means "Child of God" — so are the bad ones also the Children of God, or only the good ones? The Patriarch fixed his spellbinding eyes upon me, he weighed me up lovingly in those coal-black pupils of his, and after some weighty deliberation he said . . . The bad ones are . . . also the Children of God . . . I bowed to him and I went out into the yard, all a-glitter with snow, and the monks were standing now in the turrets and they began to set the bells rocking with great blows of their paw-like gloves, mittens like goalkeepers wear for ice-hockey, and the bells pealed out in harmony over several miles of snow-covered landscape, over Moscow and surely further still, the bells hung in the open Romanesque windows of the tower, and the figures of the monks moved in rhythm, contrapuntally, to the bidding of the blows of those ice-hockey mitts . . . The Deacon came across the yard, and women knelt, and he blessed them, and he gave them the cross to kiss . . . I knelt down too, and he blessed me, and when he gave me the cold silver cross to kiss, he saw the label on my coat lapel, saying where I was from, and he said quietly . . . You can talk Czech with me, I was at the seminary in Prešov . . .

So the bad ones are God's children too, Dubenka, they and all of us are Emanuels, it was for us that Kant wrote that little book . . . *Zum ewigen Frieden* . . . "On Perpetual Peace . . ." Dubenka, that was the wonderful time in Moscow when during the summer a seventeen-year-old German student landed his plane in Red Square, it was the Day of the Defenders of the Soviet Sky . . . The tiny plane crept in close to the ground like a wolf . . . He flew in past the streets of Moscow — steering himself neatly over a bridge above the river, he slipped his craft in under the trolley-bus wires, and the policeman directing the traffic in front of the Kremlin managed things so well that the plane made a safe landing, it only bobbed up ever so gently against the red Kremlin wall . . . And as the young man leapt out, two women carrying bouquets to place on Lenin's tomb, seeing that child dressed as an airman, gave him their flowers, because they thought it was all part of the display for the Day of the Defenders of the Soviet Sky . . . Dubenka — those women, the traffic cop, that boy pilot, all of them are God's children . . .

And likewise, Dubenka, this year in Prague — during those January events about Jan Palach, that child of God who burnt himself to death in 1969, finding no other form of protest against the August invasion of his country by the fraternal Warsaw Pact forces — I too received my share of tear-gas at the foot of Wenceslas Square, moreover I was accorded the honour — when radio reporters started asking questions like, What's your reaction to these hooligan provocations on Wenceslas Square? — of being able to say to a reporter child of God . . . You've come to the right man here — my whole life and poetics are based on three Russian hooligans . . . the writers Seryozha Yesenin, Vasily Shukshin and Vladimir Vysotsky! What hooligans are these? That's what I said, Dubenka, to those radio children of God, so off they went to find some other sons of God for their microphones . . .

So anyway, Dubenka, I reckon, when a good person dies, to be rewarded in heaven, the soul is transformed into a dove, like the Holy Spirit descending as a dove upon the Virgin Mary or the Apostles at the time of Pentecost. And when I saw those thousands and thousands of dead pigeons and doves in the Budeč rotunda, for me one of those doves was my wife Pipsi, who was so long dying that in the end she became a saint . . . I remember how back in Kersko, three days before she asked me to take her to the Bulovka Hospital, she suddenly asked me to go up to our "signal box", to the veranda, and fetch a particular number of *World Literature* . . . I felt anxious . . . Where was I to look? But she said to me softly . . . It's lying up there, I was reading it only yesterday, there are planks and boards on the cover, as if they were making a scaffold for the front page . . . but ah . . . Three days before Gary Cooper died of cancer, he asked for a silver cross and then just to be left in peace . . . My Pipsi died on the third day too . . . those last days of her life, when she looked at me only twice, never before had I seen her so beautiful, so youthful, so full of Heaven and sky . . . And twice in that time, maybe only twice during our whole life together she said to me quietly, beautifully . . . Thank you, Bohoušku . . . Thank you, Bohoušku . . . My little dove flew up from the rock . . . And now I know, Dubenka, that she flew off over Sokolníky, across the river, to that place where the doves have flown to die for centuries — to the dome of the rotunda . . . to where Wenceslas would ride out to visit his grandmother Ludmila, later strangled with a long white scarf . . . And Dubenka, who knows how this 21st of August may yet end?

I remember, Dubenka, when you were in Kersko, you wanted

to pay your respects to my wife . . . So we drove over to Hradišťko in my white Ford, to the woods past the village where the memorial is, to my family, whom we exhumed from their graves in Nymburk and put in a collapsing beer crate made of oak from the Polná brewery . . . We went into the cemetery, and here's the memorial, done in the style of Moody, a rough-hewn stone with a round aperture, like the one dreamt up by Hieronymus Bosch, the picture's in Venice, a gigantic tunnel through which the dead fly into a dazzling bright light . . . And there, beneath that tunnel, I left you, I went to the pump for some water . . . and when I'd pumped an empty pickle jar full of shiny water and turned around, I had to stop in my tracks . . . There you were, Dubenka, kneeling before the mound and bent forward, both arms plunged up to the elbows in earth, touching the pebbles with your brow, because the whole of our grave is sprinkled with pebbles, brought back by my wife from all the seas where we bathed, and where she was happy, because my wife loved bathing, I used to call her my little sea otter . . . And when I came back over, Dubenka, you were quiet, still up to your elbows, still with your knees in the stones, your brow leaning over, imprinted with the sea pebbles, merging still with that which was mortal in my wife and shone out from her urn and from the other urns too — while for more than a year my wife's soul had been in Budeč in the dome of the rotunda . . . in heaven . . . in the form of feathers and tiny bones . . .

Dear Dubenka, when the snow falls, we'll go together to Moscow — Moscow is so beautiful when it's breast-deep in snow! Again my Dřevíkov monastery will hang from the skies, tons and tons of material, looking like something made of crepe paper!

Round and round we'll go, and back again, round and round the Kremlin in a ring! Peter the Great too, and Ivan the Terrible, both were God's children, Immanuels . . . But we'll go to this Dřevíkov monastery, and we'll buy four bunches of flowers, the young people are queuing up already by the cemetery entrance, putting on their mask of grief, and the moment we go in, there he is! There he lies at the gate, Vladimir Vysotsky with his guitar, and the horses rearing over him, at his feet there are thousands of flowers, so beautiful in that deep snow! And those sad mourners! Children, Immanuels of his, who loved him and thank him now, assembling their pebbles in the snow . . . We give thanks that you lived and will live with us for ever . . . And, Dubenka, I wept . . . And, Dubenka, I wept a second time, when I saw the marble memorial to Seryozha Yesenin . . . those armfuls of flowers, and his giant blue tomcat watching over misty blue Russ . . . his "curly head of mine" and "moonlit evenings and grey-blue night, once I was young and all was different quite . . ." This is where we shall go, Dubenka, and I shall recite all his verses to you about the moon — all his bird-cherry and birch, and Anna Snegina his unhappy kulak woman . . . We'll go up and bow, and honour his mortal remains with a bunch of flowers — Shukshin's there too, lying under a perspex lid to stop the flowers from catching a cold — we'll lift up the lid and hop inside, into the warmth of the flowers, gazing at the photo of that drunkard — another brilliant writer, we'll bow at those remnants of red guelder roses, standing guard at his head . . . They say, when he died unhappily, the guelder rose was in flower in Moscow, so his coffin was sprinkled high with red guelder roses . . . for Russian poets are prophets, rhapsodes . . .

Then we'll take the last bunch of flowers over to another memorial, a huge one, black and marble and convex like those mirror surfaces with a ten-metre diameter . . . Dubenka, will you be able to make out what it is? That's the fall of Icarus, on the left, in gold, and on the right there's a golden face, Lenin perhaps? you might say, but it's not . . . it's a memorial to Tupolev, designer and builder of jet aircraft . . . but we'll only give him half the flowers, the rest are for his brother — none other than Yul Brynner, from that film *The Magnificent Seven*, their parents came from Kamchatka . . . and they had such a tremendous party in Moscow when they visited each other that people still talk about it to this day . . . So we'll visit this Dřevíkov monastery, Dubenka, and we'll bow to Vysotsky — who, when his wife took him to Hollywood, was introduced with her in the film club as "Mrs Vlady accompanied by her husband" — whereas by the time they left the Hollywood restaurant, and Vysotsky had borrowed a guitar and played and sung for two hours, it was "Vladimir Vysotsky accompanied by his wife" . . . We'll bow to Yesenin, who shot himself, and hung himself too, to make quite sure, in the Hotel Angleterre . . . Let me tell you the story, Dubenka, of how once the Hotel Angleterre caught fire during the German bombardment in the Second World War, and that fire in the sacred hotel had to be put out first, before the firemen went off to deal with the government buildings . . . Dubenka, the Russians are so devoted to their rhapsodes, their poets . . . once after they'd taken me to a big party we went silently out into the country, and there amongst some houses on a hill slope my Russian hosts suddenly took off their fur caps, clasped their hands together, and I said, What's this? And they told me with feeling that this was a place where Pushkin had once sledged . . . Dubenka, in the end all of us are the children of God . . . But who knows what's in store for us this coming 21st of August. What will they get up to this time, these angels from the tiled Bartolomějská nick?

I think it was Hana Bělohradská, Dubenka, who lamented the passing of the sixties in words something like this . . . "And so the age of Antonín Novotný the Good passed us by, that age when the arts flourished, when there was a new wave in film, a new wave in literature, and a new wave in thinking in general, and we didn't even notice — it was the era of Papa Novotný and we weren't satisfied, we wanted something else . . . And now we've got it . . ." It's all so sad, Dubenka, all those fine young men who emigrated . . . Kundera's an emigré, that playboy who knew how to write and to talk, and when he walked down Národní třída, all the girls turned their heads, but so did everyone that appreciated Czech literature . . . and Forman's gone too, that ornament of Prague, his film *The Firemen's Ball* is on now in Prague cinemas, and the young audiences shriek with laughter, bowled over by what they see on screen, as if that Forman film had been made only last year, specially for them . . . Where are the times when our leading critical journalist Ladislav Mňačko would walk over the Charles Bridge with a beautiful girl, bearing a bunch of roses? — Mňačko, author of *Delayed Reports* and *The Taste of Power*, a handsome Slovak, who always knew how to dress well and wore smart ties — gently he would brush the girl's elbow, and people would turn their heads, honoured by the sight of this almost loving couple. Now he lives in Austria — while often he gazes from his apartment window through a telescope at Bratislava Castle, needing no entry visa for that . . . And lastly, where is Eduard Goldstücker, "der schöne Edó", as they called him? that admirer of Franz Kafka, who wore Budapest and Viennese fashion and whose curly hair shone with brilliantine . . . And lastly, too, where is Viola Fischerová, blonde poet, and muse of Prague poets? for whom, as she passed in the company of dark-haired Egon Hostovský, men's eyes would open and close in admiration, before and after — where is she? We know the answer — for where is the man who wrote that book *Spooks for Every Day*, that terrific author Karel Michal? He emigrated too, taking Viola as his wife, but he couldn't adjust to exile, and shot himself in bed beside her . . .

And who will take the blame for forcing the poet Jiří Kolář to move his chair and table to Paris from the Café Slavia? Jiří Kolář, who for more than a quarter of a century delivered to his friends at midday all that information about poetry and the trends in the art world? Who will take the blame for making this fine man depart from the centre of Europe — that founding member of the Bohemians Fan Club, who always stood at Slavia football matches behind the goal beneath the clock in his casual gear? He that was proud to be a qualified carpenter, yet had the status of a polymath?

Dubenka, all this came about because the era of Papa Novotný passed us by and we failed to appreciate how lucky we were, as Hana Bělohradská lamented . . . Where's that internal emigré, that still handsome man Sasha Kliment, known as le beau Sasha? He comes to the Myrtle, now and then, only about once every three months — he who was once so outspoken in public, has had his courage drained out of him . . . just like that lovely couple, the dramatist Josef Topol and Věra Linhartová, poetic beauty and author of *Speech Despite*, she who, back in the days of Antonín the Good, recalled those South Bohemian carved madonnas — long, long ago she stopped drinking to drown the sorrows of emigration, and there in Paris, like the beatniks before her, she plunged into the Pacific sensibility of the Japanese, and now she writes her poems in the speech of samurai and geisha . . . Where is Pavel Kohout, once the adornment of every public talk and discussion? back in the fifties a committed Communist poet, standing there on May Day beside the first Soviet tank to enter Prague and put a full stop to the Nazi occupation. Where's that lovely man with eyes like Charles Boyer? He too resented the age of Antonín the Good, and now he's in exile, he who took up such a thoughtful dramatic stance, his hand in his overcoat pocket, beside that tank beneath the Kinsky Gardens . . .

Dear Dubenka, and as for Havel, along with Kliment one of the *enfants terribles* of the time of Antonín the Good, as for Havel, who was also one of those fine young men of Papa Novotný's era, I'll tell you about him once I get started on describing my journey to the Delighted States, just at the moment I'm still thinking about those words of Hana Bělohradská, that the era passed us by and we hardly even noticed how lucky we were . . . Then August came along, that twenty-first of August nineteen sixty-eight, when the exodus began, the loss of our fine young men . . .

"I'll leave my native soil behind, unable to overcome my sad sorrow, become instead a wandering vagabond . . . Through the countryside I'll roam, looking for the simple life, till one day a friend pulls from his boot a knife . . . Through the countryside I'll walk alone, seeking for a gently warming sun — the one whose name I say o'er and o'er, she will drive me from the door . . ." I recite this bit of Yesenin to you, Dubenka, with one or two slips, just as I recited him in Moscow, in the Writers' Club, in a restaurant like a freemasons' lodge, full of dark timber and balconies, dark wooden railings and stairs, they showed me where Seryozha Yesenin used to go and sit, they showed me where he got into a brawl, and fell over the railing from the first floor gallery, head first on to the dance-floor, but he got up unscathed, everyone was shocked, but Sergey got to his feet and went back to fight on, he ran up the steps and fought on like a true hooligan . . . Then I recited these verses I'd brought along with me in my head from Prague, translations I know from the nineteen-thirties, from a volume entitled *Misty Blue Russ* . . . "And though you be drunk by another, yet your eyes' fatigue still remains, and your tresses' glassy smoke . . ." and . . . "Moonlit evenings and grey-blue night, once I was young and all was different quite . . ." and that long poem of his youth . . . "No more to ramble in the crimson bushes, or trample the goosefoot, searching for your track . . ." I found out that his Isadora Duncan, she had three children, and one day when she was bathing in the sea, she saw the car move off and roll down into the water with the children inside, right before her very eyes her own children drowned . . . Yoy! And I found out Yesenin was an emigré too, an emigré at home, forbidden to speak and read in public, his blue-misted Russian poems removed from the libraries . . . I found out that about two years ago they made a film in Moscow called *War's Coming the Day After Tomorrow* . . . about a girl in the Stalin era who recited some forbidden verses by Sergey Yesenin and her teachers made such a fuss, she went and committed suicide . . . Yoy!

I don't know, I don't know if the Patriarch of the Orthodox Church is right to say that all people are God's children, all of us Immanuels . . . that even the bad ones are God's children, even Papa Stalin . . . Maybe, perhaps . . . Who knows? Allowing for *coincidentia oppositorum . . . et les extrêmes se touchent.* Aha! Yoy.

Dubenka, I'm sure you're wondering why I'm so keen on quoting these Russians, why I think of myself as living in a practically Soviet republic. You see, I recognise the *status quo*: that the political situation can't be altered, everything that has been done cannot be undone, which means I live in a land of limited sovereignty, as they said to us in that unhappy year of nineteen sixty-eight, after the twenty-first of August — a time which is now rising again from the dead, but I am shocked and scared and horrified at this, I don't want anything to happen here, to give the armed angels from the tiled nick a cause to intervene . . . I was always a man of the *status quo*, but at the same time I'm a man who wishes to have his *modus vivendi*, to be able to say what is the essence of literature, to express my own *glasnost*, my own view. Not that I would pay for it and pay anything for it, but, as Hašek taught me, being a man of the Party of Moderate Progress, that is my *modus vivendi* in this Central Europe of mine, this literary laboratory from the first four decades of this century, where I feel myself to be walking in the footsteps not only of Jaroslav Hašek, but also Doctor Franz Kafka, in the footsteps of what Ladislav Klíma wrote and stood for, the writings and the attitudes, the affinities to Prague of Richard Weiner, Franz Werfel, and Rainer Maria Rilke . . . Artists who knew how to go against the grain . . .

Dubenka, there is so much in these relationships between the people I live with — so much yet to be written, so much concealed as yet in the conscious and subconscious, so much elucidated by Sigmund Freud in *The Future of an Illusion* and in his theory of laughter and the realm of anecdote — which is typically Central European, and especially typical of Prague . . . Dubenka, here you have it, this is my *modus vivendi*, my heart's *status quo*, this is my mode of thinking and especially writing, because I'm a writer, and, being just even a tiny bit ashamed of this calling, I constantly say of myself, that I'm more of a recorder, more of a literary reporter — as well as a lover of mystification — and as for my palavering, that's my defence against politics, my policy in fact — my mode of writing.

I'm writing this after a dreadful night, when I was kept awake by the eclipsing of the full moon, all night I kept wrapping myself up in the sheet and unwrapping myself again, breaking out more and more in a sweat at the thought of what I'd been reading about in the papers, those dreads prepared for the twenty-first of August . . . I so much wish for no Night of St. Bartholomew, no Night of the Long Knives . . . I've drunk a quantity of Russian Stolichnaya vodka and my no longer curly little head is tingling with it . . . I've become a hooligan.

Dear Dubenka, today is Friday. When I went off into town, people were going home already, having more or less been told to leave work at midday and stay away till Tuesday morning, for the times were bad and could be even worse, if they turned up to work on Monday the twenty-first . . . I've gone all neurotic as well, the women next door, who listen to Radio Free Europe and so on, are putting ends of cucumber on their foreheads, to keep their nerves at bay — this Friday feels to them like Good Friday, the women have gone nuts, they think it's Easter, with Easter Monday to follow, the day when young men traditionally lash the girls with wands of willow . . .

When I got out at the Museum, I noticed how the young people were sitting around the statue of Wenceslas again, it was blazing hot, and it looked like Italy, a constant forty in the sun . . . and street-sweepers were sweeping, street-cleaners in orange vests . . . and as they swept beneath the feet of the young people sitting on the chain round the hooves of St. Wenceslas, people were admiring them, they said, how nice, we haven't seen such careful young street-cleaners round Prague for a long time . . .

Then we sat in the Myrtle drinking, while editorial folk came in, complaining facetiously about how they too had to go home and stay away till Tuesday morning . . . We sat on in the pub, and the mood was neurotic, the laughter evaporated, and eyes had shifted slightly askance, away from that Good Friday and on to the coming Easter Monday, that day of traditional lashings, crucial to the future not only of Prague, but also of Central Europe . . .

So we had our beer, and our talk moved on to the Habaners, those Anabaptists, famous for their pottery, and all of them giants, basketball players to a man, travelling through Moravia, on into Slovakia, and across into Moldavia, practising their glazed pottery, decorated without human figures or faces . . . They came from Berne, in Switzerland, expelled for religious reasons just after the time of Wycliffe . . . I said, thinking all the while of Easter Monday — forty years ago I visited the place, it was the six-hundredth anniversary of the Swiss Confederation, founded so that there would be no more dreadful bloodbaths, as in the time of Wycliffe, who wanted to exalt human relations . . . There on the lake I saw millions of children's paper boats, floating with candles wherever the wind would carry them, in honour of having put an end to all these Easter Mondays, Twenty-Firsts of August, Nights of the Long Knives and Massacres of St. Bartholomew . . .

Somebody opposite me said — to avoid like me having to think of that coming Monday — how he'd just delivered some Habaner ware to a Geneva bank, twelve floors down into a vault where the riches of the world lie, including the gold bars of Reza Pahlavi . . . And now, Dubenka, a huge collection of Habaner ware will lie there as well . . .

And behind me in the Myrtle a man leaned over and he whispered . . . Do you know who our greatest collector of Habaner ware was? And he answered right away . . . Mr Havel senior, Václav Havel's dad, he bought the precious pieces from Prague antique dealers during the First Republic . . . I said, That's a nice one, because Havel junior has just been broadcasting and appealing on Radio Free Europe and America for anyone who was a friend of his to stay at home and not go out this Sunday evening and Monday, in order to keep the peace, if only for a little while, but peace nevertheless . . . for he was also anxious about this Easter Monday . . .

Then two young men came over, and one said this friend of his was visiting from America, he'd read my book published there, and could he take my photograph? . . . so he took my photograph, and then he enquired whether I couldn't exchange a few sentences with him, exchange a few views — we could speak Russian, because although he lived in America he was actually Russian . . . And I said . . . Bugger off, will you, for one thing, I can't speak Russian, for another, in two days' time it'll be the anniversary of the day you Russians came to Prague and turned the place upside down, just like your Russian alphabet . . . so piss off out of here, or else speak Czech . . . But he just kept on saying how he'd like to talk Russian, so I got an interpreter to tell him where to go, to where we and our businessmen have been since nineteen forty-eight . . .

So they left us alone, and we went on discussing, and began to grasp, why the Habaner folk went off with their women and children and their common exchequer to Moravia, and subsequently to Slovakia, then into Moldavia and back again . . . why Prince Ditrichstein, on being summoned by the Emperor to Vienna and advised to wipe out the Habaners, objected, saying they had such beautiful pottery, they were God's own children for the arts and crafts . . . Then they agreed — and half of the Habaners were hung, and their womenfolk raped by the pandour soldiery . . . but the remainder regrouped, they no longer wander about Moravia, they've emigrated to Canada, and remnants of their priceless artefacts lie in the twelfth vault of the Swiss National Bank, next to the gold bars and other treasures of the Persian Shah, who died of cancer somewhere in Cairo, intestate — and so this Habaner ware will end up as the property of the republic which, six hundred years ago and more, set up the Swiss Confederation, in order to put a stop not only to more Nights of St. Bartholomew, and Nights of the Long Knives, but also further Twenty-First of August anniversary atmospheres . . .

As I came out of the Myrtle, Dubenka, I saw a little group of decimated doves and pigeons toddling about . . . and coming the other way an old woman pensioner, one of the pigeons wanted to beg something off her, but the woman gave it a kick, feathers flew . . . and I yelled out . . . Good grief, you wretch! What do you think you're doing? Can't you see the dove is a messenger of God? The old girl took a fit, she fell flat on her back, just like First Lieutenant Lukáš when Ensign Koťátko reported that his batman Švejk was waiting for him in the office . . .

Dear Dubenka, during your first visit to Prague, you said things in Czech which drove us wild . . . Mr Hrabal, this lavatory woman yelled at me . . . Shut the door, got a fucking pole up your arse or what? And I said it was the general custom, amongst ladies minding public conveniences, loo-ladies, to imagine they ought to have been secretaries . . . And then, my dear Dubenka, you surprised our table beneath the little antlers saying . . . Folks, I went to see Mandlíková play tennis, and d'you know what she said when she flunked the ball? . . . To jsem to posrala! — I buggered up! Is it okay for me to say that? So Mr Marysko said . . . Lassie, we say it all the time — and where did you hear it? And you innocently said . . . In San Francisco . . . But, my dear Dubenka, while I remember it, Mr Marysko, who christened you Dubenka instead of April, he's dressed himself in the guise of a grey dove, and he's flown off to the other side of the river Lethe, over to Budeč, to the dome of the rotunda, where the tiny bones and feathers lie of all those dovesses of his who went there before him . . .

P.S.

On the 21st of August I sat in the Tiger with Mr Hübl — we'd sought refuge and sanctuary in here like they used to do in churches in the old days, because no-one was supposed to be killed in church, and no-one ought to be arrested in the pub. Once when I took a look outside, about a hundred young people ran past the Tiger clapping — Mr Hübl sat there chain-smoking and miserable, worried he might be taken and held in custody, but he wasn't, so he just sat there and drank and smoked an awful amount, while I sat opposite him reading, I could hear his heart, his thoughts — maybe he was thinking, like me, that perhaps it would be better if we both just kicked the bucket, it's all a bit too much for us . . . Then Mr Hübl, distant father-in-law to the late Mr Marysko, smiled, he put off dying for the moment, and said: Are you coming in tomorrow for a beer? What do you say, dovey?

27th August 1989

P.P.S.

As the intelligent reader may have noticed, Wycliffe in the text should be replaced by Calvin (and that too with a pinch of salt).

A Few Sentences

Dear Dubenka,

You're Ariadne, and I'm Theseus, you're unwinding a several-thousand-kilometre-long thread, I'm in a situation described for me by Mr Marysko — I'm the Ten of Diamonds, that image of a bear with a chain in its nose held by its keeper . . . Well now, for two whole months I had all my papers ready in Prague, only the American airline, Pan Am, just wouldn't hand over an air-ticket — I went there every day, till it was Thursday, and I, who was supposed to be wound on to the reel by you in Stanford on the following Saturday, was still a non-starter . . . So I drank, I drank inordinately — after all, I was supposed to fly out from Prague on the Saturday, and those two ladies in the office on Pařížská just kept shrugging their shoulders at me, while down in Vienna Susanna had all her bags packed ready, the Swiss friend who was to interpret for me during my trip around your Delighted States . . . So, like a true Slav, I drowned my sorrows, drinking anything wherever I could. It was Friday before I got the tickets, and I felt such joy, that I went straight out and got drunk, and I was met by Pavlová the painter, who gave me a bottle of Myslivecká, Huntsman's spirits, to wish me happy hunting in the Delighted States . . . And I asked a girl in the foreign section to come up to Sokolníky the next morning with a car and give me a lift . . . I slept badly. And I packed only the barest essentials, as if I was only going off for the weekend, and in the morning I drank a spot of that Huntsman's spirits — and then when I went out in front of my tower block in Sokolníky, I sort of stumbled and fell face forward on to the pavement kerb, I had a kind of black-out — just about broke the thread you'd begun to wind up right here at the starting line . . . And my eye swelled up, and I was, well not actually in a state of shock, it was more that I was still drunk or maybe I was drunk again . . . The beautiful girl from the foreign section wrung her hands over me, I'd gone and torn my new trousers, but I carried on regardless, I was shaken and bloodied, but still smiling — so, like that bear on the Ten of Spades, like Theseus, with that signal tugging at me from thousands and hundreds of miles away I set off for the early morning airport . . . Heeh-heeh.

Six months before my wife Pipsi died, Dubenka, she too started to be wound up on to a long, long thread . . . I was right beside her and I saw that thread, I heard it, it was as if that thread passed through my own heart, as though it passed through my own nostrils, all you had to do was twitch it, tug it a little, and now I understood what a wee horse felt like having the bridle placed in its mouth every morning — and then the coachman twitches at the reins, just as the ride requires, yuy!

Dubenka, forgive me this digression, these days I'm being nothing else but constantly distracted from my path, so don't be surprised if my writing sometimes veers off course like a horse veering to the near or the off side, sometimes I'll even go backwards, like my poor old brewery stallions had to be able to do, like horses the whole world over . . . And now as I'm writing this to you,

Dubenka, I have to tell you that when she was dying, often my wife would say to me there in the Bulovka Hospital, right in front of other visitors . . . Go home, go home, go and change your shirt! And I would go home to put on a clean shirt, happy that my wife was giving me a dressing-down in front of the other people at her bedside in the Bulovka Hospital, and glad that she was still telling me off, just like she used to when she was fit and well . . . But once she said to me there in the hospital . . . I'd like to go home. And I said . . . But where to? Back to the flat? With a shifted gaze she said . . . No, I want to go home. I said . . . To Kersko? She shook her head . . . Where then? To your sister's in Schwetzingen? I said. But then my wife became tearful and she said . . . No, where my father is . . . I said . . . He's in the cemetery, near Heidelberg . . . No, I want to go up there, up there to my home . . . So said Pipsi my wife, and then a miracle happened, she improved, the idea of Heaven raised her up from her bed, and she returned with me to Kersko for many weeks to come, we even flew to Cyprus . . . but I knew it, I could see it, wherever my wife went, through her and through her whole being it passed, wherever she turned, that thread passed, upon which death was slowly but surely drawing her in . . . it passed through her liver, it was like a rope and chain binding a little dog to its kennel for the rest of its days . . . Sometimes, Dubenka, when I'm sitting in the Hook, the Myrtle, the Green Laboratory, that place where we used to sit and drink our Krušovice 12° beer, I meet a friend of mine in a state of shock, he's missing three fingers — last year during the cold frosts, he saw a little doggie left out on the balcony of the apartment block opposite . . . so he started making him a little kennel . . . but just as he was finishing off the final board, the circular saw slipped, and he cut off three of his fingers . . . As soon as he was better, he went round to deliver his kennel, but they told him they didn't need one any more — to stop the little dog from having to suffer in the bitter cold, they'd had it put down . . . Yuy!

So I boarded my plane, Dubenka, and off I flew towards Frankfurt, and whenever in my state of a hangover I gave a little twitch to your thread, I could feel right away how I was being wound on, how the peg you'd started to coil up our journey round was safe in your twisting fingers, and I felt like Pipsi my wife, I knew that I was in good hands, nothing could happen to me, because I was flying home, to Stanford University where you live — invited by a dozen or more official letters, in which these various universities of the Delighted States confirmed that they were expecting me on certain dates, these invitations are little flags demarcating the route and boundary lines of my university slalom . . . When the plane landed at Frankfurt Susanna was there waiting for us — she was horrified by the sight of me, for my eyebrow had swollen up so badly that on looking up I could see the overhang of bloody skin — she gave me a good telling-off on the spot, right away we had some beer, and right away she said to me . . . For goodness sake, what kind of a crazy idiot is that Dubenka of yours? She's been ringing up already to ask where we are and whether she oughtn't to fly over to Washington to meet us, don't you think she's a bit off her head? And that was a good sign, Dubenka, I could feel it in my nostrils — how at the other end of the gigantic thread you gave it just a tiny little twitch, and I found that that my swollen eye and my shocked brain were able to respond even through the air to the fact that we're together in harmony, like the Greeks taught, you and I are two halves, separate halves which long for one another and merge in the end into a single whole . . . But it was at Frankfurt that my hangover really got started. When we boarded the Lufthansa plane, and I saw the uniforms, seeing as I'd just been reading the biography of Admiral Roeder, I got the uniforms mixed up, and on boarding the aircraft I yelled out, Heil Hitler! . . . Susanna apologised for me, and everybody excused me, because they saw what was clear for a fact, that I was drunk, Dubenka, but what was the cause of that? The authorities had issued me all my papers two months ago, but the Delighted States of America had only sent me my ticket one day before my departure. And that hurts a Central European, and so, because I'm a Slav, I admit I did drink a bit, and the painter woman gave me a bottle of Huntsman's spirits, to wish me happy hunting . . . Later I fainted, and ten kilometres above sea level they gave me oxygen, and I was amazed to find that though I thought I was flying to America I was being addressed by officers of the Heerswaffe . . . I was truly shocked . . . What would Dubenka have to say about that? . . . And Susanna shouted . . . She's just as crazy as you are, if she comes to meet us in Washington, I'll hand you over to her and fly straight back . . . But you didn't come to meet us, Dubenka, it was night, and I was so worn-out by all that waiting for my air ticket to the Delighted States that my right leg had gone numb — that's my *hemiparesis lateri dextrae*, from the time a crane fell on top of me in Kladno in fifty-two, after which my writing got better — So now I couldn't even walk, Susanna got me a wheelchair, the kind they have for travelling invalids, she sat me in it, and as we rode off, I was so worn-out by that waiting about in Prague for my air ticket that suddenly out of the blue I started yelling like Hašek's Švejk . . . To Belgrade, to Belgrade! Then we got to the parking lot — and there was the writer Arnošt Lustig, after some hugging and kissing we were loaded into an American car, and what talk and what joy, friends together again after so many years . . . And Arnošt Lustig said to Susanna . . . Could I ask you something? Ever since yesterday Mrs Mládek, with whom you'll be staying, and I, we've been rung up morning and afternoon by this woman April Gifford, asking if you're here yet. And Susanna exclaimed . . . It's that Dubenka, it's that crazy woman again, this is going to be some trip to America! I remonstrated with her . . . For goodness sake, if it hadn't been for Dubenka, we wouldn't have enjoyed such a fine beginning, such a lovely start . . . ah, if only Jack Kerouac could see us now, if Dylan Thomas could see us now . . . and Jaroslav Hašek . . . Hah-hah!

Dear Dubenka, seeing as you're a student of Czech, I have to tell you this, I read through Hašek's *Švejk* again at one fell swoop, it's even more brilliant than I thought, it's brilliant because it was only when Hašek had almost forgotten about the war, only then, in the process of re-evaluation and playful rhapsodic improvisation, did he write a book that was pure, the style of writing is transparent, glazed, translucent like Empire furniture, it's written as though he tossed it off with his left hand, after a hangover, it's pure joy in writing, the true *Fruitio Dei*, only in the declining days of his life was he able to write what he did, when he could say, I am what I am — it's what the poet Otokar Březina dreamt and spoke of, that drunkards and mystics have a lot in common — like you and I, Dubenka, you who wanted to travel those three thousand kilometres and more to meet me, Arnošt Lustig said you even wanted to come on your bike in that inclement weather, to ride your bicycle! You're a crazy woman, as Susanna says, so please don't do it! You'd probably catch your death of cold. Hašek's *Švejk*, now that's real glazed writing, translucent, transparent, artless literature. But Dubenka, the main thing is, don't come to meet me on your bicycle, I was horrified that day we arrived at Meda Mládek's with Arnošt. What a surprise that was for Czechs and lovers of Czech literature . . . Ah, Dubenka, that glazed Hašek, practically at the end of his life, dictating his magnificent *Švejk* to Mr Štěpánek, it's in a whole different league from Hašek's first published book of stories from 1912, which is just second-rate humour. *The Good Soldier Švejk and Other Strange Tales*! It's like the difference between my first Haňťa in 'Baron Münchhausen' and the later Haňťa in *Too Loud a Solitude*!

And Dubenka, to show you the perpetual growth not only in colloquial idiom but also in local slang . . . Yesterday in Prague I took a cab, and as we made a swift U-turn, swerving across an unbroken white line, the cab driver said . . . If the fuzz saw me, they'd bag me on the spot — he used a word for bag or cull — they wouldn't just fine me, they'd take my papers to the cleaners . . . So, not only a bag or cull of partridges, or hares, or a bag of pheasants, but even a cull of taxi-drivers . . . And so it is!

In Washington, Dubenka, we stayed at the house of Mrs Meda Mládek, still a great beauty, and her husband, who has wonderful eyes and wonderful clothes, he's a real gentleman. They had invited guests the night we arrived, Mrs Lustig was there too, and I was drunk, not only was my eye swollen and shut, but I had a smashed-up forehead and a rip in the knee of my new hard-currency trousers. It was supper time, I looked about me, there were pictures by František Kupka all over the walls, and through the open doors I saw into other rooms and corridors, cats were walking about and dogs lying around — all the guests who'd come to welcome the famous writer were taken aback by my appearance, so in order to make conversation Mrs Meda Mládek said . . . Susanna, this afternoon a student of Czech called April Gifford phoned from Stanford to ask whether you'd landed and how Mr Hrabal was feeling . . . or rather, she called yesterday, because she'd mixed up Friday with Saturday . . . Susanna exploded . . . She's crazy, that woman, she'll drive me round the bend . . . So Mrs Meda Mládek gave a signal instead, and two young African girls, Moroccans to whom Mrs Meda spoke French, brought in trays of ham, while I drank my beer from the bottle, not even noticing I was sitting next to a beautiful Czech woman, with her husband opposite, all of them just beautifully dressed, but so taken aback . . .! And all I could see were these pictures by František Kupka hanging on every wall, I saw them totally super-distinctly, both the colour and the drawing, because I was drunk — well actually I had more or less sobered up, but now I'd fizzed up again after two bottles of beer! Susanna described our journey to everyone, I was shocked by what I'd done, by what I'd been getting up to, but I smiled and said . . . This is about first times . . . When Dylan Thomas flew to the States, he was drunk too and he looked like an unmade bed . . . but it's lovely here, may I take a look? And I got up and walked from one Kupka to another, and Mrs Meda was gratified, and to cover up their embarrassment, the guests began talking about literature and so on . . . And I walked down the corridor to the library, the whole wall was glazed, outside was a yard with a stout tree-trunk, and another house, also glass all over, and a swimming pool with soft beige lighting and blue tiles . . . two metal rotors turned on the ceiling, gently agitating the tender beige steam, and I saw a metal spiral staircase worming its way up to the ceiling, topped with a little balcony, also metal, and from it a black metal door led to an attic, or a little room, or another apartment. And seeing this, Dubenka, I forgot how worn-out I was, I went back to the company of people, cats and dogs . . . and everybody was eating and talking at the same time about Václav Havel, about the rights and wrongs of him being in prison . . . And I squeezed a slice of ham in my fingers, I lifted my head and dropped the ham into my mouth, I ate with relish, and then I said . . . You see, it's like this with Havel: He's revived two myths, the myth of Socrates and the myth of . . . oh, who was it stole the fire from the gods? . . . It'll come back to me . . . Anyway, it was for insulting the gods and corrupting youth, like Havel — né Václav — that Socrates was condemned to death. He said, it was better to obey the law of the land than to go into exile, the choice he was offered, so he drank the cup of hemlock, even though he'd have preferred, rather than drink that cup, to be nourished for the rest of his days in a public institution . . . And likewise Václav Havel, who, though offered the choice of exile too, prefers to obey the law of his land, and so, my friends, at present he's in jail . . . I said these words to mark the inauguration of my stay in the Delighted States, and having a lovely voice, hoarse and fluey, I gained their attention — then I had some more Pilsner from the bottle and I added . . . Now I remember, Prometheus it was . . . the other myth renewed by Václav Havel is that he, like Prometheus, stole the fire from the gods — not that the eagles are gouging out his liver now, but it's because of that stolen fire that Havel — né Václav — is sitting in jail . . . It's only logical, isn't it? I sat down, missing the chair and spilling beer down my chest, so I got up again and protested . . . It's nothing, nothing . . . When Dylan Thomas flew into New York, with his bundle of luggage . . . for breakfast he had a double scotch and soda and he said — Christ, the heat, I nearly evaporated on the flight . . . And the passengers? A bunch of glaring, sullen, frightening runts, international spies and Presbyterians . . . And you aren't doing any better . . . Mrs Meda smiled sweetly and her husband got up — a huge tomcat leaped up on his shoulders, curled round him like a fur collar — and Mr Mládek bowed, he went over to a round wall, pressed a button, and a door opened in that round wall, Mr Mládek went inside with the tomcat, and the door didn't close, but Mr Mládek went up in that lift . . . Mr Mládek's ascension to heaven . . . soon only his knees were left, then only his shoes — after that nothing else in this country ever astonished me . . . Aaaaaaah!

Dubenka, it was both awful and magnificent, even though I was plastered, I could still feel clearly that you had me there on the end of your great long thread, we were still communicating with each other through the air . . . I was taken through the library by someone, then out into the damp fresh air of the yard, in front of us lay that swimming pool brightly lit with an orange light . . . Someone took me carefully across the blue paving and tiles at the edge, then drew me by the hand, up those spiral stairs, someone else was pushing me from behind — but the three of us wouldn't fit on to that little cast-iron balcony, and the door in the wall wouldn't open, there were too many of us, so one of the Samaritans had to go back down the stairs. Above our heads the two metal ventilators whirred and spun, if you'd craned up a bit too much, the metal rotor-blade might have scalped you . . . Finally we tumbled into the room, and when the light came on, it turned out to be a flat, a bedroom, a bathroom and a kitchen, with terrifying sculptures along the walls and heaps of wire, even a gleam of glass . . . I fell into bed, some kind of metallic statue shape reared up by the wall like a suit of armour squashed flat — human hands laid a cold compress on my gashed eyebrow, and then I fell asleep . . . I always fall asleep right away, as long as I'm drunk . . .

Ah, Dubenka, I've just remembered, I have to tell you before I forget . . . A few months ago they invited me to the French Embassy for dinner, something to do with the French offering increased opportunities for students and the like to visit France. The Ambassador made the offer, hands outspread, saying it was the 200th anniversary of the Great French Revolution . . . then an official from our Ministry of Foreign Affairs replied, thanking him, but saying we didn't need any help with revolutions or *Liberté Egalité Fraternité* . . . on the contrary, we were so far ahead that France, if she so desired, could benefit from our good advice and experience, for we had already brought in socialism, so he thanked him . . . And reader, at this point the Ambassador's outspread hands of friendship withered . . . so I got up myself, Dubenka, I tapped a teaspoon against a glass, and I thanked the pair of them, but I said that seeing as I was here too, I'd just like to say that in my view literature, and especially Czech literature, generally has to work against the grain, ruffle up the society in which it lives, go against the nap, know how to strive for the forbidden — it's even true, as I learned from Rainer Maria Rilke's *Malte Laurids Brigge*, that sometimes it's better to keep certain texts hidden out of sight round the corner, it's better to lead a fuse up to them, and then, at a certain point, you light the touch-paper and run away from the contents — for the texts dearest to me are those I wrote in such a way that they scare me, they frighten me, and I reckon, Mister Ambassador, that it was French literature taught me this, for France is my second home, and Paris is my second city of birth, Paris is dear to me as Prague is, and inspiring . . . So I said, Dubenka, and it brought me invitations right away from the ambassadors of six different European countries, who'd been invited to this celebration of the bicentenary of the French Revolution . . . Who would have thought it . . .?

Dubenka, at the lovely Mrs Meda's, up there above the swimming pool, I just caught the sound of them letting down the window blinds, and the blinds on the doors, I heard the blinds coming down in my head as well, and so from all sides, outside and inside, I fell into unconsciousness — the only beautiful thing about drunkenness is that state of unconsciousness, that *tabula rasa*, that silence and nothingness, that non-being, when you really get a proper rest, at the price of a hangover the next day . . . But my unconsciousness here in Washington was suddenly illuminated by a lamp, a light which hissed like a gas lamp — probably this was because over there on the other side, on the beginning or end of the thread that joins us like an umbilical chord, as a kind of conception without ejaculation, suddenly I was full of the light of your face — just like once when we sat at some candle-lit tables where hundreds of flowers blazed, in Kersko, at someone's birthday party, in the evening amongst the flowers and the tipsy — pleasantly tipsy beautiful young women and men, we sat together at the head of the table, it was lovelier than if it had been our own wedding, actually in a way it was our own wedding and our wedding night . . . And now I leapt up, Dubenka, there above the bathroom and the swimming pool, but I struck my hip on something, and fell over backwards on to the bed — I tried again, and again I was caught by this sheet of metal, I cut myself again, till finally I lit the table lamp, with its two bulbs which were surely two-hundred watts apiece . . . I didn't know where I was — I knocked over the two shining milky bulbs, and there close to the wall was the culprit, that squashed flat metal armour-bearer, by now the bed was covered in blood from my hip and shoulder, I tried to get up and again I fell over in a backward somersault . . . finally I managed to totter on all fours into the bathroom, I rinsed the blood off my face, and staggered over to the door, just about gashing myself on a lurking window pane sticking out of some kind of sculptural assemblage, I turned the door handle, and the black door swung open and unhinged itself — so there I was holding the handle and hanging over the blue swimming-pool, with the beige steam rising, the two iron ventilators revolving, and there I was hanging legs down, holding on to the door-handle — Dubenka, have you see that Charlie Chaplin film called *The Gold Rush* where he hangs on to the door-handle of the cabin over the abyss? There I teetered, but because you, my guardian angel, were standing by, with one more kick in the air I swung back towards that veranda, and suddenly I was standing there and looking down — I'd never seen anything as beautiful, as super-real, as that which I saw below — those tiles, that fresh gushing water, those two ventilators and that fearful spiral staircase, like a helix . . . And Dubenka, as you are a student of Czech, I'll tell you, how right Mr Roland Barthes is when he says . . . *seuls les évidents sont stupéfiants! Nur das Offenkundige kann verblüffen* . . . I'd landed safely under your direction, you tugged on the thread as if it were a bridle, and you led me back to my attic apartment . . . where meantime my pillows had caught fire, set alight by the two-hundred-watt bulbs . . . so I picked them up, singeing my eyebrows, I took them to the toilet — a good thing I'd inspected the place first! — and I stuffed those burning pillows into the bidet and turned the water on. And it was beautiful, so beautiful, to see those burning crests of pillows and white linen, as yet untouched by the flames . . . Then I collapsed into the bed made ready for me by the lovely Mrs Meda, that saint who eternally smiled, even at the way I arrived, and all that happened, including the things she didn't know about yet, everything pleased her, the way I turned up there like Dylan Thomas . . . I lay there, unable to sleep any more, because I'd noticed something that always gives me the creeps, this audible presence, this cotton-wool filling my room and kitchen, the air conditioning . . . that quiet, sinister purring, that appliance which is worse even than the bugging devices in the palaces and residences of Prague and world diplomats, embassies and international hotels, here it was, and I was supposed to drop off and sleep, here at Mrs Meda's, whose voice, I remembered lying here in the bed and in my blood, was

such that when she spoke down in the dining-room, no-one inter-
rupted, only her beautiful insistent voice spoke, always about art,
with which she seemed totally spellbound — like the sound of a
million coins pouring out of a slot-machine, coin after coin cas-
cading after a lucky break into your joyful cupped palms, till all the
million coins are emptied out . . . that was Mrs Meda's way of talking, pausing for a while only to start off all over again, because art,
conversation about art and art itself is infinite . . . So I'd introduced
myself, Dubenka, and I'd represented Central Europe, and Prague,
its heart . . . and my Jaroslav Hašek, who his friend Mr Longen
writes about so beautifully . . . Heeh-heeh heeh-heeh!

Deciding to get up, unable to believe this was all true —
ungumming myself from a bedsheet caked with dried blood — I
looked in the bathroom mirror and gave myself a real fright, I was
horrified, and when I saw the charred pillows, feathers the colour
of burnt sugar jammed into the bidet, I just wished the ground
would swallow me up — someone, probably Mrs Meda, had
already put plasters and bandages out on the table, I fingered again
those metal plates above my bed, but through the slits I could see
it was now light outside, so I pulled up the blinds, the venetian
blinds . . . and I sat on the bed, making my usual lengthy inspec-
tion of my fingers and feet, which mercifully distracted me from
any thoughts about what had occurred, about what I'd done to my
hosts . . . What can I say, Dubenka? As they wrote of Dylan
Thomas . . . Dylan drank his own blood and sucked his own mar-
row, in order to reach his own essence . . . But what kind of essence
am I heading for, Dubenka? I've got to do something about this
drinking, I've got to, because I'm starting to get dt's, and that's

bad, girlie. Even if it's only for your sake, Dubenka, I've got to sort myself out a bit — I mean, you didn't just send yourself over to Bohemia, you didn't just waltz into the Golden Tiger from San Francisco all by yourself, you didn't just take the Saturday bus out to Kersko on your own, you didn't just send yourself out into Central Europe — you were *sent* . . . It was your destiny, and now here am I sitting in Washington, I've hit the bottom and I'm determined, not just that I will — but that I *must* begin a new life now, just for your sake, for you, working in that department store over in Stanford and teaching Russian in the afternoons, just so as to make a living, to feed the little dog you found, the little bitch you wrote to me about, who sleeps in your bed . . . I remember how this crazy tour of the universities all began, I remember how you settled down under a great birch-tree in Kersko, you propped up your head with that little blue rucksack with its five-kilo Czech-American dictionary, and you smiled, you smiled like that woman in Nezval's poem 'The Drowned Woman of the Seine', you wanted nothing, you had no wishes, it was enough to hear the leaf of the birch-tree rustle up above and feel the heat of the shining sun — I sat down beside you, I didn't look you in the face, I couldn't, because you would've seen how fond I was, how much I loved you . . . Then my cats came and surrounded you, five of them all sniffling you, you offered them your fingers, and the kits half-closed their eyes and felt you, the littlest one even snuggled into your lap, but you looked up through the leaf of the birch into the sky, with unblinking eyes you saw, sketched out in advance, in Kersko, my whole tour of America — you saw Woodrow Wilson University in Washington, then further into the blue sky you drew the blue line on to Columbia University in New York, and on — we mustn't leave this one out — to Cornell University in Ithaca, then I have to stop off in Detroit and lecture at Ann Arbor, Michigan, and of course you drew your blue thread onward to Chicago, to the university at Urbano, and naturally I have to see Nebraska, where you were born, where your mother lives with your six siblings, at the university in Lincoln the film curator Dan Ladely will look after me . . . and what if I visited Harbor Front and in exchange for my lecture they took me to Niagara Falls and the Six Iroquois Nation Reserve? Then the university in Boston, where it rains all the time, I'll have to take galoshes and an umbrella . . . then on to Los Angeles to see the beatniks . . . You dreamed, and then you recited to me your dreaming, and with a little map you sketched it all out with a blue pencil over the United States, this Kersko dream of yours, imagining all the places I'd visit — you said you'd written to the universities already, not only was I going, but I absolutely had to go, so that finally I would land up in San Francisco, at Stanford University . . . And you asked me what I thought. And seeing as this was all for next year, I said to her, yes, YES! Because I didn't hope to be still around, I used to think about how it might be better not to live, rather than be without my Pipsi . . . YES! I cried out that day in Kersko, and now I'm sitting here — and you're at Stanford University, there's a thread in your fingers and you're winding away at my anabasis, my pilgrimage, my *On the Road* by Jack Kerouac, that bus journey across the continent from the Atlantic to the Pacific Ocean. But meanwhile, Dubenka, I'm still here, worn-out and smashed-up, afraid to go downstairs to the Mládeks, after being such a terrible guest . . . I opened the black door, and what met my eyes? Steam, pink steam up to the ceiling, the two black ventilators revolving slowly at the ceiling, and the blue pool below — where Susanna was swimming naked, that was her thing, wherever she was, she had to bathe for the sake of her spine. The ventilators slowly turned in the pink vapour, lights shone from the ceiling, it was like mixing apricot ice-cream . . . And Susanna swam on her back, naked and pink, like a peony, and calling up to me . . . Hello! Come and have a swim too . . . What a night, and so you've had a good sleep . . . But now! That daft Dubenka's rung up already to ask how you slept! Go to hell the pair of you! You're in love with her and she with you! Go to hell the pair of you!

Ah, Dubenka, you've jumped your Thurn-Taxis Ditch, your Beecher's Brook, the Atlantic! When I got the air-mail packet, the several dozen invitations from those American universities, I saw, Dubenka, how your unshakeable talent and courage had obliged you to make that leap, and even when you saw that watery ditch, you still landed on all fours, and now you ride on to the finishing line, where you'll be waiting for me, at Stanford University . . . Then, when it was my turn to jump the Thurn-Taxis Ditch, not only did I fall into the watery ditch, I just about broke my two legs, I just about broke my neck. And now I'm sitting in the watery ditch, I'm just picking myself up, ready to carry on, there's nothing else for it, tomorrow I'll put on dark glasses, a plaster over my eye, and I'll go to my reading at Woodrow Wilson University, my discussion with students of Czech and anyone enterprising enough to ask me about my life, my literature, my views about the world . . . In actual fact those university lectures of mine were just like talking to you! After all, we're linked by that blue thread, by which you draw me on to the shore of the Pacific Ocean, so that what I'm going to say tomorrow, I seem to be saying to you today . . . For me our Grand Pardubice Steeplechase is not only a symbol which stands for something completely different — for me not only this great race, but especially this Thurn-Taxis Ditch is a cipher which I find able to enlighten for me not only human life, but the whole world . . . For me this Thurn-Taxis Ditch represents a boundary-situation, as Karl Jaspers taught me, because what I am, I am drawn into, not only by my own destiny, but also by my own will . . . Jaspers teaches us that the signa of existence are: freedom, decision, choice, communication, obstinate will, devotion, absorption in oneself, opening up to the world, conversion, absolute consciousness, mood . . . and love . . . Dubenka, how that Grand Pardubice race with all its obstacles and ditches and fences, how it corresponds to our own lives, our own living and thinking. What a Thurn-Taxis Ditch separates the child from the adolescent, the boy from the youth and the youth from the man, the girl from the young woman and the young woman from the wife and the wife from the mother, and the man from the father — what ditches these are that each person must leap, ditches you jump only once in your life, ditches whose jumps cannot be taught, for even horses jump the Thurn-Taxis Ditch only once a year, and every horse is so scared, it only dares it again a year later because it's forgotten about it in the meantime . . . I hope, Dubenka, that I really am on the other side of the Thurn-Taxis Ditch now, that I can ride along safely, led by your thread, all the way down the marked course to the finishing line, where we'll meet again . . . I wonder if you still have the red ruby ring I gave you when we said goodbye at Florenc metro station?

Dear Dubenka, I send you my greetings, these few sentences, I put my two fingers on my upper lip and with an upward motion, as along the diagonal of a letter envelope, I send you my greetings, the kind sent by children flying their kites, holding tightly on to the string — they love to send little messages up to the kite in the heavens. I wanted to send you a photo from last year's Karlovy Vary film festival, of me shaking hands with Bertolucci, I have to tell you about a young photographer who wanted to take my picture — I said, we'll meet on the balcony after *The Last Emperor*, it's sunny out there . . . So we met, but just as he was getting his camera ready, a television crew came past, and they went over to a spot with a view of Karlovy Vary from the balcony, and suddenly, what did I see? but Bertolucci coming down the long balcony, so I said, Look here, is your camera loaded? You're about to get a good one, okay? Right you are, Mr Hrabal . . . So I went up to the famous director and I offered him my hand . . . saying in my broken French . . . Mr Bertolucci, I was so enchanted by your film, and even more enchanted by your press conference . . . and Mr Bertolucci, your eyes, they aren't just your eyes, they're the eyes of Charles Baudelaire . . . So I said, and I could see the young photographer wrestling with his gear, and Mr Bertolucci, as if he was aware of this, leaned over to my ear and whispered to me in French the first lines of Baudelaire's poem 'Une Charogne' . . . Rappelez-vous l'objet que nous vîmes, mon âme, / Ce beau matin d'été si doux . . . Then he shook my hand and walked over to where the TV crew were standing . . . and I said . . . Have you got it then?

Oh, Mr Hrabal, I could jump off the balcony on to the cement, my camera's gone and buggered itself . . . I said . . . Look now, lad, just keep your cool, Mr Bertolucci's got to come back, hasn't he? And that goes for you too, Dubenka, over in San Francisco — keep calm, be patient, and in the end, just like the child's message travelling up the twine to the kite, the further away I get, the nearer I'll be to you . . . That'll be some reunion, yuy!

Just a few more sentences . . . So Bertolucci came out again, and I got up and said . . . Mr Bertolucci, I'm a Czech writer, some of my books have been published in Italy, if you give me your address, I'll send them to you, okay? . . . So Bertolucci wrote his addresses, and the photographer laboured away smiling . . . Then we said goodbye . . . And I said, Right, did you get it then? Yes, Mr Hrabal, I did . . . So I'm sending you the picture from the newspaper, dear Dubenka, and before I forget — I have twelve cats altogether this autumn, tabbies, toms and kittens, and when I get out to Kersko, I trip over the beasts, but in the end I feed them all the same and I give them milk, and then, since thinking of you gives me kittens, I sit down to write you a letter. The leaves are falling outside, the sun is shining, and the birch-trees have already dropped their leaves, letting the sun shine through their top twigs, and it's so beautiful — just like that beautiful Indian summer in New York where I sunned myself a quarter of a century ago by the Atlantic Ocean listening to the bell on the buoy chiming its death knell to the thousand kitties left there on Coney Island beneath the pier, and nobody came to them, so they slowly died, except for a couple of brave ones, who had the courage to go across the beach and steal something from the humans . . . but here in Kersko there are so many fallen leaves, if you were here you could easily lie down again in the leaves warmed by the sunlight, lean against a birch-tree, prop up your head with your matching blue bag, your little rucksack blue as the sky, with its five-kilo Czech-American dictionary . . . It's such a beautiful autumn here, the leaves fall, and as the days pass every leaf is ever more colourful and translucent, every little birch leaf is so tender, like cigarette tobacco, like cigarette paper, in the end it grows so light and silky, it scatters in a light waft of a breeze, the whole crown, the crowns of these birches of mine scatter, like Liszt's *Liebestraum* for the piano, the middle part, where the fingers have to range over the whole keyboard, up and down and left and right, just like scattering the leaves of the Kersko birch-trees . . . The cats and kittens play, they leap and catch those falling postage stamps that signal the end of summer, its symphonic climax, and the rainy, muzzy, depressive days of late autumn will come and the onset of winter . . . Yoy! And one day when the snow falls, Dubenka, we'll go together, just you and I, to Moscow, we'll hire a car and drive out to where Boris Pasternak the poet lived . . . outside Moscow in his dacha, he lived in a countryside like Kersko too, birch-trees and pine, and he had a field, where he grew potatoes like me — but then we'll go to the cemetery he found for himself, there even if the snow is up to your chest the path to his grave will be swept, there's a stone, sticking up like a milestone, and in it in an oval a relief of the poet's face, Pasternak's profile, done by a certain Moscow sculptress after Anna Akhmatova's verses . . . And his face was like a Berber and his horse . . . Ach!

Dubenka, I wanted to add just a few more sentences about my

tour of the Delighted States, but I'm still full of this recent signed document called 'A Few Sentences' . . . a sort of sequel to Ludvík Vaculík's 'Two Thousand Words' of 1968 . . . We're back in Prague, in Central Europe, where thousands of people have signed 'A Few Sentences' . . . and those few sentences have become the acid test for those in favour of rigid dogma and those in favour of creative dogma, I mean those who wish for change in our political and hence also our cultural life. And what a fuss there was, protests, accusations saying I was a collaborator, just because I didn't sign 'A Few Sentences' — I was even honoured by a visit to the Golden Tiger by kind Václav Havel, who'd written me a note, saying he wanted to come and see me, but I'd left, because I was having dinner at six with a friend, and Václav only got to the Tiger after seven — and my friends became enemies, when they looked for me in the Tiger, they even shouted . . . Where's that collaborator? And I preferred to be this collaborator, because, Dubenka, as I also said to Václav Havel that Saturday afternoon when with a thousand other people I celebrated the anniversary of the French Revolution in the gardens of the French Embassy, I said to him . . . Yes, Václav, maybe that day in the Tiger I would have signed it, but not any more. And why? Because I wouldn't swap that signature on 'A Few Sentences' for eighty thousand copies of my *Too Loud a Solitude*, due in November, I won't swap 'A Few Sentences' for the eighty thousand afterwords by Milan Jankovič . . . I mean, Dubenka, the only purpose of my being in this world has been to write this *Too Loud a Solitude*, that *Solitude* which Susan Sontag in New York said was one of the books, the twenty books that would form the image of the writing of this century . . . So I didn't sign, just as I didn't sign 'Two Thousand Words' either, not that I wouldn't have signed at the time, Vaculík even came flying through the office of *Literární listy* with those 'Two Thousand Words' and he said . . . Bohouš, give me your signature on this . . . And he gave me a pen, and I would've signed those 'Two Thousand Words' like a blank cheque . . . but Vaculík suddenly said . . . Don't sign anything — but in the next three days write me something about Truth . . . So I wrote my 'Play for Truth' . . . and in the end that essay replaced my signature, just as my 'Magic Flute' replaced my signature on 'A Few Sentences' . . . Heeh-heeh-heeh-heeh.

19th October 1989

The White Horse

Dear Dubenka,

So here I am in New York. I, son of Manhattan now, I Bohumil
Hrabal, I cosmos of Prague-Libeň, here I am, to pay my respects
to Walt Whitman, who went about in a wheelchair at the end of
his life, and still managed to teach the young man who pushed his
royal poetic throne how to write poetry. Here I am, I've just arrived
from Washington, that capital city whose streets radiate off through
the suburbs into the countryside, into the valleys of leafy trees,
where brooks gurgle, and across them lie felled tree-trunks, to let
everyone see what the end looks like, not only of trees, but of all
things. Now I'm in New York — I've been to the Bowery, and a
bit further on, to the main avenue, with its Banks of all Banks —
it's a fantastic place, this city, where they show children who won't
study how they'll end up like drunks dying on the street . . . and
right next-door lie the capital deposits of the Delighted States . . .
And here, Dubenka, I sailed round the Hudson strait and river with
Susanna . . . it was misty, and the skyscrapers towered, waist-high
in that tender mist, and our boat followed the line of the shore,
and once again . . . how lovely those skyscrapers are, how breath-
taking in their picaresque assemblage — up where the mist begins
the office lights were shining already, such a tremendous sight,
those lights up there, almost where the sky begins! And another

tremendous sight, along the shoreline round Manhattan there's a wire fence, a kind of belt around Manhattan, a zone of at least five or ten metres, where everything glitters that the city no longer requires — it's as though it was all done specially by Kurt Schwitters, with the assistance of Robert Rauschenberg . . . Here in that confusion of dead and discarded things rats slip and slither with slimy bellies . . . and boys have their own Eldorado, their own kingdom here amongst the bushes and brushwood . . . theirs, but also mine, for I myself as a boy loved all those dells and dumps of refuse at the back of St. Vojtěch's Church, where they carted off everything that people didn't want, had no further use for, things that were outmoded . . . dead and buried . . . And out on those avenues and streets, what fine limousines driving by with ladies' knees on the back seats, what beauty, those American automobiles and their drivers, driving, not by the highway code, but eyeball to eyeball, sharp eyes ever decisive at the crossroads — crossroads glittering with sharp eyes — the driver only carries on along the main avenue when he detects assent in the eyes of the person entering from the sideroad . . . And out in the suburbs, what beauty, Dubenka, motor-car graveyards, flattened automobiles, that have served their time, grown obsolete, antiquated, and outmoded . . . Of course it's not only New York, every city in the world displays the same juxtaposition of life and death, the maternity hospital and the funeral parlour . . . but here in New York the rhythm of life and death just hits you right in the eye . . . Here come elegant men and beautiful women, and here below them at knee level are the eyes of those who beg, holding out empty tins — it doesn't matter whether it's a woman or a man sitting there, white or black, each receives a token coin, and when the nickels have accumulated to a certain point, the beggars get up and go to their drinking dens in their own streets, and when they've drunk whatever they begged, they come back and sit where they sat before . . . It's a tremendous city, Dubenka, with tremendous collections of modern art and any old sort of art . . . the staff in the museums wear lovely blue uniforms, just like the one I had myself, working on the railways — in summer I had a blue lustre jacket — what's more, all the staff have patent leather shoes, and most are black women, especially attentive to their appearance . . . Dubenka, I'm so beside myself with this city, I'm no longer particularly interested in my lecture at Columbia, or the publication of my book *I Served the King of England* by Harcourt Brace Jovanovich . . . It was nice to find that Susanna and I were staying in a Methodist hotel just a little up from the mouth of the Hudson, where all that Robert Rauschenberg and Kurt Schwitters stuff lies about on the shore — that little hotel of ours in Greenwich Village, Dubenka, now that is just perfect! For three days in a row I went to a small pub serving Dutch beer on tap, and for three days in a row I couldn't get enough of those beautiful, dead-beat, smiling black girls, serving food and beer with big, fixed, V-like smiles, smiling all the time, as if they wanted me to marry them. It was lovely in that little pub, Dubenka . . . I didn't even care about Susanna yelling at me every day at the publisher's or in the hotel . . . To hell with you, you and that Dubenka of yours, she's rung me up at the hotel again, she's phoned the office at Harcourt Brace, to ask if we've arrived, if Mr Hrabal is feeling any better yet, and whether I'm looking after you properly . . . And, Dubenka, I confess to you repentantly — I did start looking after myself — and since the lowest death rate is said to be found in public houses, I spent as much time as I could in the White Horse Tavern . . . And only on the third day did I cease gazing at the girls' knees — college girls who come in, throw off their coats, and sit and study here, with their lovely legs neatly crossed . . . on the third day, it was, I discovered I was sitting at the window where Dylan Thomas used to sit, I saw his portrait in the corner, painted in oils, with a red nose, which suited him well, but anything suits a drunkard . . . And there opposite was a polished bronze plaque, and on it — Susanna translated for me — something like: If you talk of your childhood, speak quick, if you're slow, I'll interrupt and talk of my own, Dylan Thomas . . . Then another plaque, which Susanna didn't have to translate: Richard Burton.

So there I sat, Dubenka, in the White Horse, with the black girls serving food and beer, above me they kept a little ashtray, and in it a cigarette, and as they swept past me, each had time for just a little drag, and they brushed a breast right up against my eye, just like Věra and Vlasta in the Golden Tiger, years ago, properly brought-up barmaids in those days — they too, before they laid fresh beers on the tray, would rub a breast up against my eyebrows, and I, Dubenka, then as now in the White Horse, every time I purred with ecstasy. So there I sat, meditatively, the black girls took their intermittent puffs, and I was sitting right where Dylan Thomas used to sit, till the drink gave him delirium tremens and he died three days later in New York's St. Vincent hospital . . .

Then came the real thunderbolt, Dubenka. Andy Warhol! That exhibition for which people queued up as if for a basketball match, so many wanted to come and see what I too came to see . . . Andy

Warhol, who reached such a height of emptiness and everyday-ness, who said this to everyone: "What's so great about this country is that America started the tradition where the richest consumers buy essentially the same things as the poorest. You can be watching TV and see Coca-Cola, and you can know that the President drinks Coke, Liz Taylor drinks Coke, and just think, you can drink Coke, too . . ." And I'm proud, Dubenka, that his parents came from Miková, near Medzilaborce in Slovakia, Andy Warhol's eyes are the eyes of Ruthenians, melancholy eyes — the eyes of peasant muzhiks, who drink from despair at how short life is and how a poor man has nothing but his honour . . . And when it was our turn, Dubenka, we went into the huge foyer of the Museum of Modern Art, and there we saw several hundred cows with halters, several hundred cows adorning the walls like wallpaper, and all at once I realised — that before the Campbell's Soup there had to come these cows and their meat . . . What we saw later were all familiar things — we'd admired them before, but we'd never attached such importance to them . . . till Andy came along with all those Liz Taylors, and Jackies, and all those car crashes, and Elvis Presleys, and soup cans, and plane crashes, all those dollar bills and hundred-dollar bills, and electric chairs, in short, everything that surrounds us in this city — but it was only when Andy Warhol took his Polaroid snapshots and enlarged them with his silk-screen technique up to two metres or more, only then did this really express what attracts us in human misfortune and beauty, in those champions of film, theatre, sport and public life . . . in discarded things and people, all this material we can't take our eyes off, in newspapers and news reports and posters — Andy Warhol caught us in a trap of our own making, and he gave art a whole extra dimension . . .

Then it was my birthday, and Hanka arrived from Palestine, a Jewish lass who, after my lecture at Columbia, had offered to take me out for my birthday treat — she invited me to a posh fish restaurant, down by Pier 17, where the boats leave for their trips round Manhattan. I requested, Dubenka, to be allowed to celebrate my three-quarters of a century at the White Horse instead, saying I had Dylan Thomas's table there, and they were all invited . . . But Hanka with her chutzpah insisted on going to the fish restaurant — it'd be a real surprise, she said . . . And it was, Dubenka, it was, they had food all right, but no licence for beer, customers were supposed to bring their own . . . so Hanka brought along some Sapporo in white bottles which looked like milk, but it was worse than that — it was warm . . . So I celebrated my three-quarters of a century with warm flat beer . . . and we ate à la carte all the best top restaurant nosh, but what was the good of that, when over at the White Horse they had black waitresses and cold Dutch Heineken beer on tap . . . which tasted a bit like our own Popovice Bock . . . That was some surprise, Dubenka, it truly was . . .

On the Saturday afternoon, before I gave my lecture at the Sokol Hall, Mrs Jovanovich offered to take us wherever we liked . . . I'd just seen *The Unbearable Lightness of Being* at Arnošt Lustig's flat in Washington . . . that film based on Kundera where sex rules the world, and all of a sudden, smack bang! the Russians arrive in Prague, shown in documentary film from the time by the Czech director Jan Němec . . . so I wanted either to see that Kundera film again, just for those five minutes . . . or else Chaplin's *The Circus*, seeing as Arnošt and I had gone out every day to hire one of his films . . . *City Lights* and *The Gold Rush* and *Monsieur Verdoux* and *A King in New York* — but we'd missed *The Circus* because it wasn't in stock . . . Well, Mrs Jovanovich found out *The Circus* was playing at some place near the Sokol Hall, so off we went in a taxi . . . only, after Mrs Jovanovich had leaned into the box-office, she turned round and said smilingly, Sorry, it's not on today, seventeen Russian directors are here to show their films and have a discussion . . . So Mrs Jovanovich took us instead to this place where they settle film contracts, where New York artists meet, Bob & Kenn's . . . It was dark in there, but TV screens glowed from the walls, a softly-lit billiard table stood there, greenly gleaming, and lovers were sitting, and customers like us, eating . . . Everyone was staring at one of the TV sets, basketball was on, and basketball for Americans is the tops, it's their sporting pop-art . . . One basketball player, his name was Jordan, was playing in his last match, and as a going-away present his fellow players and pals had bought him the most expensive English car, a Rolls Royce . . . That was quite a man, Dubenka, that was some player! He was from Washington and he scored differently from all the others. Each time he magically caught the ball, which kind of hesitated in his pink palms for a bit, he went round his opponents with his bent smooth-shaven head, then suddenly he thrust up, with those hands, and that leap of his — and the ball just swung into the net . . . Everyone was enchanted by this black player Jordan — of whom Susanna said he always scored more than half the points in any match . . . So we'd exchanged *The Circus* and the Soviet film directors for Jordan's last match at Bob & Kenn's . . .

I was also meant to meet Philip Roth, who had captivated me with his book *The Ghost Writer* and made me hate my own writing . . . but when we got to the office, Dubenka, there was a note saying Mr Roth was sorry, he'd buzzed off some place . . . But one day Susanna and I went to visit Susan Sontag, that finest contemporary woman and writer — famous for her book on cancer, *Illness as Metaphor* . . . You went down from the street, into a basement area, and there was a door, a handle offered like a handshake, a passage, and then a room just like mine in Kersko, and when the lady who led us down the passage turned, I saw it was she, Susan Sontag, author of that book about cancer, and presently engaged on a new book: about AIDS . . . She invited Susanna and me to take a seat, and sat down opposite us — a giantess with beautiful eyes and a mane of hair, branded at the front with a silver streak . . . We were quiet for a moment, then she asked me how the journey was, and whether we'd like coffee or tea . . . Then she smiled and said, that novel of hers, which I'd just praised, was actually Czech-inspired — when she was a girl, her father had forced her at first to read Karel Čapek's play *The White Plague*, but then she'd come to enjoy it, so Central Europe had actually provided her with inspiration . . . She had deep eyes, and while Susanna interpreted what Susan Sontag was saying about the new book she was working on, I saw that this lady was like the epigraph to *The Waste Land* . . . "I saw the Cumaean Sibyl with my own eyes. She hung in a bottle, and when the boys asked her: Sibyl, what do you want? she replied: I want to die." Thus T.S. Eliot prefaced his *Waste Land* . . . So I sat there with this lady, simple and wise and sad, our conversation floated about in Central Europe, she knew the crossroads of linguistic consciousness, she knew that this was what made great literature, just like Emanuel Frynta taught me by the way . . . She knew Arnošt Lustig too and his novels of Jewish suffering in Theresienstadt, she knew his story too, and I told her about how Lustig and I had sat together in Washington and watched nearly all of Charlie Chaplin's films — how Franz Kafka was an admirer of Chaplin, he'd said of him something like, "Ardent despair gushes from his eyes at the immutable lot of ordinary folk below, who still never capitulate . . ." And I told her that waiting for Lustig in Prague was King David's royal crown, a crown which I had saved when the workmen demolished the altar of the Libeň synagogue, I'd swapped that crown for a metre of beer — eleven glasses of Pilsner . . . Arnošt was going to send his sister over to bring it back, that crown which was deservedly his because of Theresienstadt . . . Then we started discussing how in America there's an influx of literature and art in general from Eastern Europe. And I said, when we had the publisher's party for my book *I Served the King of England*, at Mrs Jovanovich's, my translator Paul Wilson talked about how Leslie Fiedler called the period of the sixties to the eighties 'Postmodern' . . . but he reckoned, as a translator expelled from Prague for playing with the rock group Plastic People, if you strike off the P, that tells you what it really is . . . *Ost*-Modern, East-Modern. And Susan Sontag said, the way Mike Heim had translated my *Too Loud a Solitude* — she thanked me for it — she reckoned it would be one of the twenty books of the twentieth century. Michael Heim, a Hungarian with Gypsy blood by the way, so he's Ost-Modern too.

So, Dubenka, all this time I was in New York, I didn't bother too much about lectures at Columbia, and when I wasn't sitting in the White Horse, I amused myself watching all the scenes and images of the avenue and side-streets — and I sat at Susan Sontag's, while we played a kind of literary ping-pong together, we tried to outbid each other, we outdid each other with the names of writers and artists from the East . . . So Susan said: Marc Chagall . . . and I said Igor Stravinsky . . . she said Singer . . . and I said Malamud, appending the title I love: *Idiots First* . . . she said Philip Roth . . . and I said Josef Roth, *The Capuchin Crypt* . . . she said Franz Kafka . . . and I replied with Gustav Mahler . . . she said Sigmund Freud . . . and I replied Wałęsa, along with that new saint, Popieluszko . . . she said Wojtyla, Pope John Paul II . . . and I raised my hand, and Susanna interpreted for me: Last year the West German magazine *Spiegel* published a bestseller list . . . first place Mikhail Gorbachov . . . second by a narrow margin me . . . and Ernest Hemingway an honourable seventeenth . . . So we drank our coffee, and a wintry sun emerged, the snow fluttered slantingly down — and Dubenka, I have to tell you now, I was so cold here that Susanna had to buy me some long johns, long-sleeved underpants, as they jokingly call them in Prague . . . It was winter still, but the buds were swollen with coming spring . . . And we rejoiced that, indeed, all you had to do was strike off the P, and miraculously *Post*-Modern became *Ost*-Modern . . . Then I clasped my head and exclaimed, But we totally forgot that other *Ost*-Modern . . . Andy Warhol . . . Andy Warhol, Dubenka, a pale man with a silvery wig, born of parents who came from over by Medzilaborce, just so that one day he could hold up a mirror to this city, and this society — who studied art history, sociology and psychology, who began, Dubenka, as an illustrator, an advertising and theatrical graphic artist, who started out with huge comic-strip canvases, and during the seventies magnified those idols of American life, Jackie Kennedy and Marilyn Monroe and Elvis Presley . . . those 129 dead in a crashed jet! . . . that overturned car with five dead, and that girl's head hanging face upwards . . . that sole of a man's boot in the tread of a huge truck . . . Andy Warhol, Dubenka, surrounded by beauties, though he didn't believe in love, accompanied by guardian angels, Marisa Berenson and Lauren Hutton — beauties I dream of from those photographs by Andy's court photographer, Christopher Makos — and Baryshnikov, Russian ballet dancer in a dinner-jacket and bow-tie — that's Andy's Archangel Gabriel, photographed with him at a show — Warhol, pale and wan, shot at in 1968 by that spitfire spurned in love, Valerie Solanis, who probably worshipped him, just like Mary Magdalene worshipped Christ, so that Andy could say sex was too much of an effort, Andy, who could unite the highest with the lowest, who could take pictures with a cheap Polaroid which looked like he'd used the most expensive equipment . . . but above all Andy with the eyes of Christ, who, when his sister came to visit, used to sing hymns with her from way back there in Medzilaborce — the man I specially came to see, whose five-kilo-weight catalogue I bought, but learnt off by heart, so I could leave it behind for Mrs Meda Mládek in Washington, where I'd not only set the pillows on fire in my drunken stupor, but also left blood-stains on the bed where I slept . . .

Then, in that Castle of New York, which contains the whole of world art in a nutshell, like a kind of child's concertina book for all who study the origins of art, I remember I saw two more pictures . . . The tapestry of a unicorn, white and standing on a small islet, surrounded by a tiny gurgling stream — the unicorn has a white mane and skin, and lovely sad eyes filled with Eros . . . because only a virgin may speak to it, a young maiden, who can give birth without ejaculation, like the Virgin Mary — and that young woman is on the other tapestry, only she is allowed, and has the power, to speak to the handsome unicorn, left alone in the centre of the Garden of Paradise . . . And now I remember a third picture — the unicorn's no longer in that oval Garden of Paradise, he's running through the landscape, pursued on all sides by furious hunters, he's peppered with wounds and spattered with blood, in his eyes you see horror and dread . . . And that unicorn is really Christ, while for me, Dubenka, he is also Andy Warhol, who was shot three times by Valerie Solanis, because she adored him even more than Liza Minnelli did — I reckon Valerie loved Andy Warhol even more than his pop-star Debbie Harry did, and that's saying something . . . Of course, the one who loved Andy the most was his mum, that one-time folk artist — and he loved her too . . . Andy Warhol, saint, born in Pittsburgh, but whose parents came from Miková, over by Medzilaborce . . . Somewhere over there live the Ruthenians — and somewhere over there a Christ could be born to distribute Coca-Cola to the believers, and holy pictures multiplied by silkscreening . . . That's my Andy Warhol, a man with the face of a newly released convict, a man with a silvery grey-mare wig, whose heart is a diamond bigger than the Ritz, a man who died of heart failure, and was carried in the cabin of Apollo 8 by a 4,000-tonne thrust Saturn 5 rocket up to heaven, a pop-art heaven, and there he reigns to this day . . .

Dear Dubenka, these are words of mystification, but I may allow myself the luxury of canonizing Andy Warhol, for that is the mystery of the metaphysical moving shooting gallery, the mystery of the Puppenspiel, out of which Goethe finally, with his whole being, composed *Faust* . . . But in spirit I am still sitting in the White Horse, where the Lord's beloved Dylan Thomas sat and drank himself to death . . .

P.S.

Dear Dubenka, I'm back in Kersko now, it's misty, the little cats are drenched and begging me to let them into the warm, but I believe in the cold water treatment, so out they sit in the shed in the hay and straw, like tiny little Jesuses. And I'm watching a broadcast from St. Peter's in Rome, where the Pope has just proclaimed the blessed Agnes a Saint, Agnes, who cared for the poor and founded a convent for the poor of Prague, in the spirit of Saint Francis, who was able to converse with the birds of the heavens, Agnes, who stands cast in metal on Wenceslas Square close to the right hand of Saint Wenceslas, where people lay flowers and hundreds of candles great and small . . . Saint Agnes, that Přemyslide Princess of Prague . . . Post-Modern is simultaneously Ost-Modern . . .

Kersko, 10th November 1989

November Hurricane

Dear Dubenka,

It's the evening of the 17th November, the little kitties are all huddled up together, breathing into their paws, I went out past the white fence into the dark and starry night, and up in the northern sky a great rosy area appeared, the aurora borealis, I've seen it here many a time, the aurora borealis, decorated with twinkling stars . . . and I knew that this scarlet heavenly sign too boded no good . . . And I knew that in Prague permission had been given for a quiet candle-lit demonstration, a procession which would start from the chapel in Albertov and follow the route taken by that student's coffin, the coffin of Jan Opletal, who was shot in Prague on the 28th October 1939 by the German occupying forces . . . Up in the sky over Kersko a pink curtain was stretched, spangled with twinkling stars, and Cassius the tomcat was afraid, I held him in my hand and walked past the white fence, and I knew that this tender aurora borealis boded no good, it was a sinister omen.

What was my life in Prague like all those fifty years ago? Dubenka, I lived in the Old Town near the Law Faculty, and I too was on my way to the demonstration that 15th November, to attend the funeral of Jan Opletal, but I met a friend from the Law Faculty on Pařížská, and he persuaded me to come to the Bouda in Celetná, where we sat about drinking Budvar, and so missed

everything that happened in Prague that day . . . Later I went home
to go to bed, downstairs in the house where I lived there was a pub
called Sedmík's, and the news from the streets was bad, the atmos-
phere was depressing, — one of the customers sprinkled snuff on
the back of his hand and blew it off so as to make Mr Sedmík
sneeze, and, as he wore a wig, the trick worked and the toupée flew
off his bald pate, but Mařenka his assistant didn't laugh the way
she usually did, nor did the customers, they all sat there stiffly,
while Mr Sedmík replaced his wig, saying it was a pretty dumb joke
in the circumstances . . . And off I went to bed. The landlady was
a Mrs Olga Rissová, and she too was sad and sorry for us, — she
had three lodgers, two of us studying law, while the third was a
cook, who used to get back about midnight, roll into bed and snore
so much that I used to stuff my ears with soft bread . . . The next
day I set off to the Faculty, — I left shortly after ten in the morning, and when I got to the front steps of the Faculty, what did I see
. . . but German soldiers driving students down the steps, beating
their backs with rifle butts, other horrified students were running
out of the hall and corridors, and the soldiers herded the students
into waiting army trucks, more and more of them, then they raised
the flaps up, and the soldiers jumped in . . . I stood there aghast —
if I'd been half an hour earlier, I would've ended up like those
friends of mine, the trucks drove off, and I heard my fellow students singing *Kde domov můj*, the national anthem . . . Now I knew
what was going on, and when I got back to the house, my fellow-
student Suchánek and the cook were packing already — I packed
my things too, and we took horrified leave of our weeping landlady . . . And before we set off home to our parents, before we

reached the railway station, we could see the horror and dread emanating from everybody, and the expectation of what indeed came to pass — the closing of universities and colleges, the execution of twelve students from the 12th November, and one thousand two hundred students arrested in their student residences and transported to Sachsenhausen.

All this, Dubenka, I remembered once again this 17th November, as I walked with my black tomcat Cassius under a pink sky sown with twinkling stars, and I sensed, and therefore somehow knew, that this evening's candle-lit procession would meet with some mishap, something would happen, and I was afraid, because people arriving that afternoon in Kersko said that just up from Karlovo náměstí, Charles Square, by the hospitals, all the parked cars had been towed away in the morning, and heavy equipment of the Interior Ministry was due to come in its place . . .

Dubenka, I meant to write to you about the rest of my great anabasis, my tour of the United States, but I've had guilty feelings about not staying in Prague, not to see something which anyway hadn't yet happened, but to feel what was in the air, — all that week Prague was hysterical, disturbed, just like fifty years ago, when I was afraid as well, and thousands of students were dragged off to concentration camp, and twelve students were shot . . . and I happened to avoid such a fate, — I went to Nymburk, saw the notary, and got myself a job in his office . . .

I remember how one day during that time in Nymburk my friend Jirka Jeřábek and I went to have a few beers in the Grand, we drank a lot, and later that evening we were returning across the deserted square — speaking a sort of Bohemian Czechish mingled with German, talking away raucously and mockingly in faulty German — when suddenly two men in capes came out of the Hotel Na Knížecí with a girl, one of them seized me by the throat and roared: *Halt*! He gripped my throat, and I could see his terrible eyes, and he practically dragged me along the ground to his car . . . Just as he opened the door, still holding on tight to my throat, the girl came rushing out of the side street, K poště, and she yelled out . . . Hanzi, let the young man go at once, at once, Hanzi, do you hear, or I'll stop seeing you . . . Hanzi! Hanzi! I'll never see you ever again! And she turned and ran back into Poštovní . . . and Hanzi let me go in order to run after her . . . And I ran into Mostecká and over the bridge, I ran all the way to the brewery, because I had escaped concentration camp again, thanks to that girl, because he was Gestapo, that man, he'd have run me in for slandering the German language and insulting the German Reich, he'd have taken me to Kolín, where patriots of the Nymburk district were wont to vanish . . . And the Kolín Gestapo knew Czech, because they were Sudeten Germans you see . . . *Ich bin wetterkrank*, I feel weather-sick.

Yes, Dubenka, you wonder at my use of this phrase . . . Well, you see, as a little scholar I spent some time in the Sudeten area, Hitler wasn't around yet, and those Germans of ours in the border area were quite okay, it was the custom to go and spend a bit of time there . . . I was there to learn German, in Zwickau, I boarded with a Frau Plischke, a dressmaker, and I used to go out bathing with those Germans, we even had two girls from Zwickau spend some time with us at the brewery, Gerda Titie and Lori . . . I've forgotten her other name . . . and there in the little town of

Zwickau I used to hear those Germans say, in unfavourable weather
. . . *Ich bin wetterkrank* . . . Then they'd go for a beer and have a
wee nip of spirits with it . . . And so, Dubenka, the phrase just sort
of stuck — and when I get a bit of the old *Weltschmerz*, the world's
getting me down, then I'm *wetterkrank*, and I go for a beer and a
wee nip . . . In '36, however, Dubenka, we were in Zwickau on a
visit — by which time Hitler was around, and Konrad Henlein . . .
and those Germans of ours had changed, they were favourable no
longer, but proud and haughty, and they showed us how Hitler
was God, and their capital no longer Prague, but Berlin . . . So that
was the last time we were there, and it all ended, as you know, in
catastrophe, — Munich came along, the Sudetenland fell to the
Reich, and in March the Reich came and took the rump of
Czechoslovakia, then came autumn and the 28th October, the closing down of higher education and the death of Jan Opletal and
twelve students shot right away on that 17th November . . .
Meanwhile I had my job at the notary's, and I witnessed how, after
the attack on Reichsprotektor Heydrich and his subsequent death,
many people were executed, patriots and Communists . . . Then,
Dubenka, I got a railway job at Kostomlaty, near Nymburk, and
again I managed to elude death, the day the partisans removed
some rails near the station, and a train came through with the SS-
Waffe, and they took me hostage on the engine, I can still feel the
SS pistol muzzles at my back, and only the officer in charge of the
train, on the footplate, when he looked in my eyes, only he understood . . . he gave an order, the train stopped, he gestured with his
chin, and I climbed down the steps of the engine and walked back
to the station, and though it was spring, I was *wetterkrank* with

what had just happened . . . And three months earlier, I remember, the partisans blew up a munitions train outside the station, covered waggons, — I was standing on the platform and saw it, I felt the draught of the detonations, fifteen waggons flew up into the heavens in this practically atomic cloud . . . And then the SS-Waffe were in my office, interrogating me, their revolvers on the table next to the telegraph, but those Germans didn't shoot me, they came for me the next day, but then they let me go, I was lucky again as always, to be left merely *wetterkrank* . . .

Today is the 17th November, and the candle-lit procession of students in Prague is setting off from the Pathology Institute, from Albertov where fifty years ago the funeral procession set off with the remains of Jan Opletal . . . Today is the 17th November, it's seven o'clock in the evening, and I'm walking out with that little black tomcat of mine Cassius Clay in my arms, the white fence — its white painted laths, last painted by my wife — its white strips of wood shine upon my path, I walk this way and that, with the aurora borealis still visible over Kersko, a pink, tender and yet foreboding haze in the sky, out of which twinkling stars glow, for there's a frost in the air . . . And I think of that procession of students with candles, that officially sanctioned procession, set to wind its way from Albertov up to Slavín, the Vyšehrad cemetery, to the grave of the poet Karel Hynek Mácha . . . But the aurora borealis scares me, I fear, Dubenka, things'll work out a little different, because the heavy equipment of the Interior Ministry is waiting over there by the complex of buildings on Karlovo náměstí, and there in the adjoining side-streets stand those vans, like cages for the transport of prisoners, anyone caught in the latest Prague demonstrations . . . The stars twinkle amidst the aurora borealis, in the pink, tender and foreboding haze in the sky, while I am just *wetterkrank*, and my black tomcat Cassius is quivering in the palms of my hands too . . .

Dear Dubenka, I've just remembered how, every morning, as a boy, Franz Kafka used to be taken across the Old Town Square from Zeltnergasse, Celetná, or later from the house called 'At the Minute', next to the Town Hall, and down Týnská to Masná, Fleischmarkt, where the German school was — little Kafka would be accompanied by their hunchback maid, who even held his hand . . . And now I know why little Kafka was scared . . . in that year of 1892 Prague and especially the Old Town saw a lot of fighting and disputes between Czechs and Germans . . . so the Austrian government declared martial law . . . And then in '97 the fights between Germans and Czechs spread to the Jews as well . . . Anti-Semitism reared its ugly head again, and for the Jews it was a real "December Hurricane" . . . Middle-class Jews, Dubenka, as Theodor Herzl writes, tried to avoid the nationalist tendencies as they made their way through the Old Town . . . surreptitiously, like a secret illegal underground organisation . . . like ships tacking at sea . . . And not only Jews in general, but Franz Kafka in particular, felt *wetterkrank* with all this . . . which helped to set up the preconditions which were the sad inspiration for Franz Kafka to write his . . . *The Trial*, or the notes in his octavo exercise books, the sort of jotters used by pupils, including me, to write down new vocabulary . . . It was in just such an octavo exercise book that Kafka noted how: *One day a man visited us, a stranger, — he and my father closeted themselves in the living room . . . I was with Mother in the*

kitchen, then Father came in, pale and excited and terribly thirsty . . .
he took a drink and went back into the room to that strange man . . . and
when Father returned later to the kitchen, shaking all over he told us he
had to go off with that man he knew not where . . . I said, Dad, let me
come with you . . . but Father got dressed in a hurry, saying he had to go
on his own, the stranger would come with him, and he had to be left on
his own . . . then they left, they went down the stair, and I saw Father
going off hunched down the street and turning into the square . . . That's
the gist of that note from the *Octavo Notebooks* . . . I've given it in
my own words, because I've lost my own copy of the thing . . . actually, it's called *The Eight Octavo Notebooks* . . . That's what it all was,
and in vain did Herr Doktor Franz Kafka practise a bit of horse
riding in order to get rid of his depression and migraine and sleep-
lessness, in vain did Herr Doktor Kafka rent a cubicle at the
municipal bathing-place in order to swim, in vain did he keep his
own boat in order to reinforce his nervous constitution, in vain did
he visit the Trója Pomological Institute to hoe and tend the trees,
in vain did he go travelling whenever he could round the spas and
curative resorts of Europe — he was simply unhappy with everything around him — and in vain was he engaged to be married four
times, twice to Felice Bauer, and once to Milena Jesenská, and
finally Dora Diamant kept him company until he died — for he
started to cough blood in the Schönborn Palace, and even though
the active TB helped his writing, nevertheless, slowly but surely,
writing *The Castle*, he ended up at the Kierling sanatorium, where
he died . . .

So you see, Dubenka, what's happening in Prague now is something which has been going on rhythmically and constantly in the

past — always just a pause, a bit of time out for a breather, then *"L'ouragan de décembre"*, that December hurricane which struck young Kafka in that year of 1897, just like the events of 1989 struck us . . . And Dubenka, straight after that December hurricane, only a year later, a young girl was found in the woods near Polná with her throat cut — that hurricane continued there in Polná, the anti-Semites called it a ritual murder, they said Anežka Hrůzová's blood was gone, the Jews were guilty, and Polná's large ghetto had to be evacuated, even though the future President, Professor Masaryk himself proved at the court of appeal that it was no ritual murder, it was simply a straightforward case of murder . . . but the ghetto remains empty to this day . . .

Dear Dubenka, I take my walk, lingering at my white fence, which is white as a flying skeleton, the black tomcat runs ahead of me, romping for joy, for a breeze is blowing and driving the leaves, and Cassius Clay, my little sootie, is amused as I am not, I look up at that flitting pink aurora borealis, beautiful and foreboding, and I'm scared, I'm shocked, the aurora borealis is driving me *wetterkrank*. I know, of course, Dubenka, that over there in the Delighted States you too have had, and still have, your own hurricanes, not only December ones, — in Detroit for instance, there I was shocked to look out of the highest hotel and see how a whole downtown area was burned out, the little white train that goes round it shows you clear enough, how it was a demonstration and protest by people who burnt down an area about the size of the Old Town in Prague, imagine if this were to happen to Prague, as indeed it could, for we Czechs are touchy, hysterical and rowdy, you know . . . we like to sing, "Prague we'll ne'er surrender, we'd rather knock it down . . ." When I saw that Detroit, I immediately renamed it Destroit, a whole section of it was laid waste . . . And what happened? The well-to-do centre of Detroit built itself new villas and apartments in the suburbs, the centre was left to rot, buses go through twice a day, connecting the commercial and banking centre in the morning and bringing people back in the late afternoon, and then those huge skyscrapers are abandoned, only armed patrols watch over the empty offices and headquarters and banks, and banks of banks . . . and the old red-brick middle of town is burned out, only bare walls standing, no roofs, smoke-blackened windows, collapsed floors, blocks of weeds and shrubs where proud Detroit once stood, people strolled about, and the traffic of this automobile city was once just like New York — but now only here and there a black man comes along jogging, or a black woman, in bright coloured clothes with a cigarette stuck to her lip . . . Dubenka, remembering that city I feel weather-sick again . . . Even though the aurora borealis has now faded, vanished, and the constellation of the Wagon is shining after me — the Great Bear, and Cassiopeia, that "W", in honour of William Shakespeare, who so dramatically portrayed the lives and violent deaths of ruling English monarchs . . . Come to think of it, Dubenka, our Presidents too all have a fate worthy of Shakespeare . . . The lyrical fate of President Masaryk, the tragic fate of President Beneš, the doubly tragic existence of President Hácha, and the super-tragic fate of President Klement Gottwald, the most tragic one of all, because he was forced to have his own friend executed . . . Yoy! Dubenka, today I'm just totally *wetterkrank*. Mister Hrabal, hand on heart. It was Sasha Dubček himself handed you the Klement

Gottwald Prize, Mister Hrabal, you hold this state prize, it's for you and your wife, and after all it's the very finest Order of the Republic, this little red rectangle inscribed with a golden sprig. You don't wear it, of course, Mister Hrabal — because you're ashamed of it for bearing the name of this tragic figure in Czech history. You see, Dubenka, what a lot of trouble we have with our history, it's a constantly postponed beginning, and a simultaneous ending . . . Thus, dear Dubenka, even Mr Franz Kafka's obsessive moves were no use — he moved house seventeen times, no less — and going back to nature didn't help either, when he bought some land in Siřem with his sister Ottla — he kept running away from that illness, but it caught up with him in the end, all the way to that sanatorium outside Vienna . . .

Here in Prague, today, this 17th November, it'll be like a Good Friday, with no Easter Saturday or Resurrection Sunday to follow — and even though that pink and lilac aurora borealis has passed away from my eyes and from over me, it still remains as an ominous sign, sometimes it only takes a tiny little thing — who caused that fire for instance in San Francisco last century? The country woman who left a candle burning in a stable, or the cow swishing the flies with its tail who knocked the burning candle into the straw, so that practically the whole city burned down? In Moscow Patriarch Pimen answered my question, reluctantly but nevertheless: Yes, God's children are not only the good ones, but also the bad ones . . .

Dear Dubenka, here I am in Kersko, and the moon has risen beyond the woods — it's about the fifth day after full moon, it's cold, and the moon is like a big chunk of plate-glass window, it's gently orange, and I'm standing by the fence, while Cassius, the black tomcat, plays with the fallen leaves lifted by the late breeze of the föhn, he sticks his paws beneath them with his sharp claws, digs those agate splinters of his into the foliage — and I think of you, of that thread of yours, with which you wind me like Ariadne — and now I have to speed up these missives, these letters to you, because something's going on here in Prague, I just know it — I walked through burned-out Detroit, skirting the site of the conflagration, something must have happened there, that just had to happen, that is now threatening to happen here in Prague . . . I know, I wrote telling you how I'd like to spend this final end of my youth in the White Horse with the black lasses, those waitresses, who were so kind, really so kind, because their eyes were like your eyes, they too were probably one of six children, just as you told me you were — I wrote telling you how I'd love to sit there in Greenwich Village like Dylan Thomas, I'd love to bet on three-legged horses with beautiful names, I even said I'd forget to dress and take a bath, like Dylan Thomas, of whom the Armenian writer who met him at the airport said, that Dylan looked like an unmade bed . . . But actually, Dubenka, I like dressing up, I like alternating my various sweaters, I'd like to be good at it like Andy Warhol was, who always knew when he was being photographed, and always managed to strike a pose just like a model . . . just as I too always feel that I might be photographed, and wish that the said photograph might have that extra half of a dimension . . .

Dear Dubenka, I wanted to write you a whole series of letters, a serial, one from Ithaca, and one from Detroit, and another from Chicago, but now all those universities I've been to, Cornell,

Urbano, Ann Arbor, are sort of merging, what with this evening and the distance of today . . . the University of Urbano really struck me, but only because I made the four-hour drive there from Chicago in a downpour of rain, which lasted the whole of that journey, the four-lane highway only had a visibility of fifty metres, as if we were all zipping through thin mud which the wipers couldn't keep up with, and though it was only afternoon, we had to put on the headlamps — it was an apocalyptic ride, a journey watched over neither by angels nor by dragons, a journey that opened up curtain after curtain of thin mud and rain mixed with swirling clay, spattered by thousands of tyres, and I felt as if it was my last ride — especially when a truck crashed and mangled calves fell from it, flung about the highway verge, run over, unrecognisable, and the truck lay in that rain, wheels upturned, and two calves stood there mooing in the downpour — but on we sped towards the university city of Urbano, and the driver, who was Czech-born, comforted me by telling me the same story over and over, about cold fire, fire so cold, that Jan Palach burnt himself to death with it . . . cold fire smuggled into Czechoslovakia by the CIA, a great miracle of science, and they persuaded that crazy Palach guy to set himself alight with that cold fire, saying nothing would happen to him, it wouldn't hurt a bit, so he poured the petrol over himself and he struck the cold match, and only in the flames did he realise that the CIA agents had deceived him, for that fire of theirs wasn't cool at all, it fried . . . The irate driver was telling this tale, Dubenka, mainly for himself, as I waited aghast for us to end up the same as those calves, for our car to turn wheels up, and for us to be left standing there by some miracle just like those two terrified calves . . . But the driver only started talking again about that cold fire smuggled into Prague by the CIA, petrol set alight by a cold match . . . And then he said, you know, you come from a land where the Communists make fools of people, only die-hard Commies could believe in something like cold fire, and daily readers of *Rudé Právo*, which published all this stuff about the burning . . . Cold fire, brought to Prague by the CIA, who explained to Palach scientifically how it would only be a demonstration, it wouldn't hurt one bit . . . So on we battled, Dubenka, to the University of Urbano, and all the way through the spattered mud spray the driver went on about this cold fire and Palach and the cold match and the CIA, as it was written in *Rudé Právo* and broadcast on Czechoslovak TV . . . And I was so shocked by this ride that all I did at Urbano was apathetically read out an extract from my *King of England*, and listen while Susanna read the same piece in English, then it was question time — and at that moment the whole campus, just like the car we'd come in, was plunged into a sudden furious downpour, on top of which, as if that wasn't enough, the wind leaned into the rain, like branches of weeping willow the rain and the wind lashed against windows of the campus and the Department of Slavic Languages, whose head was Russian and enjoyed watching Susanna and me sweat for a good hour over the various questions and answers . . . Again we had Václav Havel, of course, and what did I have to say about the censorship, and the unjustly prosecuted, and persecuted, and the story of Karel Pecka, who served a fifteen-year sentence, all just for sitting in Tachov railway station, and being arrested on suspicion of being about to go and cross the border . . . I responded to all these truthful, wounding questions, trying to say I was here to discuss literature, but they said literature had to reflect life, and I'd hoisted myself by my own petard when I'd said a moment ago that Truth ought be told, whatever the cost . . . Then it was the end, and I sat there with all those Bohemists and Slavists and Russianists, and the secretary was a Czech émigrée, she asked what I did at home in Kersko, so I said I grew vegetables, and she said so did she, would I like any zucchini seeds? — she had several varieties. So we carried on for a bit with this vegetable-growing and beer-drinking, and then we set off back — by the way, Dubenka, I forgot to tell you, Susanna had migraine, she was feeling sleepy — she'd also heard that her father had suffered a slight stroke, a heart attack, so she was feeling very down — the rain had gone off by now, and we drove the four-hour journey back, with the driver still going on and on about cold fire and the cold CIA match, smuggling in cold fire and bamboozling poor old Jan Palach, insisting nothing would happen to him, as *Rudé Právo* asserted . . . I took the zucchini seeds to the Golden Tiger, Dubenka, and I shared them with Mr Hrejsa — mine died, everything dies on me now, I dug up the potatoes too and they were small, suddenly fewer than last year . . . but Mr Hrejsa's been bringing me American zucchini every Monday — ten days ago he brought me a jar of cooked ones pickled with carrot, vinegar and bay leaf, a jar with the date on the lid . . . I stood the jar in front of me, next to my beer, and suddenly in came a woman asking for me, asking if I remembered her . . . I couldn't at first, I didn't recognise her face . . . So she leant over even nearer with her glasses, brushed back her hair . . . and then she said . . . But I'm from Urbano, I gave you those zucchini seeds, did they take? And I handed her that jar of pickled sliced zucchini, and she pushed her glasses up over her brow, she took a look and she said: Yeah! They did . . . Shall I send you some more? . . . And I said yes, and let her choose a photograph of me she liked, which I signed along with a beer mat from the Golden Tiger . . . But there wasn't enough room, so I asked her to go and sit by the window, and when there was more space I'd come and get her . . . But, Dubenka, when I came back in a little while she'd gone, so we prised open the lid of the jar with a coin in her honour, and we ate those zucchini from Urbano and we relished them . . . Luckily Mr Hrejsa has her address, I'll write and apologise, for not letting her sit on my lap, in the absence of a seat . . .

Dear Dubenka, Jan Novák came to fetch me, to show me a Chicago suburb, he's a writer and a script writer, a young émigré with a beard, who graduated with a B.A., went on to a doctorate, and devoted himself to literature, he even started writing in English, winning the Pulitzer prize for his novel set amongst computers. And Dubenka, being kind of *wetterkrank* at present, just as I've been *wetterkrank* in the past, and shall be again in the future, only now do I let slip to you that it was actually Jan who drove me to Urbano — and it was I who made him tell me something out of his novel *Striptease Chicago*, about cold fire and the cold match . . . Jan and I chatted also about literature, and Miloš Forman, for whom Jan is doing a script, the story for his latest film . . . and he invited me to come and see what a Czech suburb was like. So we went to this little tavern, it was Sunday afternoon, the district's called Cicero, rows and rows of houses, a typical American working-class suburb, he said we'd go to some jazz that evening, and told me how you play American football . . . he talked about his family, his two kids, and his work . . . And Jan, maybe like all Americans, was an expert driver, more eyeball to eyeball stuff . . . And we turned in past all those little houses in their broad streets, houses with gardens, here and there a three-storey apartment block, and we stopped in front of a villa with a sign outside saying LOUNGE V. & J., a few clapped-out cars were parked in front, and the whole area exuded depression, understandably, when I compared it subconsciously to the super-rich district where Susanna and I were staying . . . An elderly man came out of the diner, under the sign saying LOUNGE — there was blood over his face, blood over his coat lapels, and a paper towel on his fore-head also soaked with blood . . . We went inside and saw the bar counter with its cabinet of drinks — and perched on a seat a young woman sat in a black leather skirt and red blouse wearing terribly thick make-up, black eyelids, sweeping eyelashes. We sat down, the blood-soaked man was there too with the waitress, who was also dressed in a leather skirt — peeling off the blood-soaked nap-kin, she anxiously inspected the gashes on his face and forehead and nose, and calmly applied another paper towel . . . What hap-pened, Dad? asked Jan Novák . . . And Mr Novák senior, I recognised him now, we'd been sitting together at a party in my honour only the day before, Mr Novák senior said . . . On the way home, at a red light on a junction, a black man ripped open the car door and tried to grab your Ma's bag . . . but she wouldn't give him it, nor would I, so he punched me one on the nose and snaffled the bag, but the contents fell out — they're lying in the car — he pointed with his chin . . . And now it was his son's turn to peel off the new, by now blood-soaked serviette, carefully inspect the wounds and say . . . But, Dad, there's another cut on your forehead, a fresh one . . . And he applied a further paper towel . . . Meanwhile the waitress brought bottles of Dutch beer — we were the only customers, apart from the doll in the red blouse with the sweeping eye-lashes . . . Mr Novák senior gave a dismissive wave of the hand, but Věra the LOUNGE manageress told the story for him . . . There was this other customer, and they started arguing about some old football match in Czecho, way back, about whether it was 'out' or a corner . . . Sparta versus Slavia . . . and as they were arguing the other guy struck Mr Novák with his fist, and he just rolled over . . . The waitress brought another one for Mr Novák, we drank from the bottle, while young Novák junior enquired . . . Who was it? And the manageress said . . . Some guy called Bican, came over from Czecho six months back, always used to get into fights in Prague, in Holešovice . . . So, Dubenka, we changed the paper towels on the forehead and nose of Novák senior, father of the famous young writer, B.A. and doctor of Chicago University, Jan Novák, who wrote *Striptease Chicago*. And we drank on and talked about literature — Jan's beaten-up Dad was one of my readers, he was pleased and chuffed to meet me, so were Věra and the waitress, who brought me various books to sign, as well as the lady sitting all tarted-up at the bar on this Sunday afternoon — no-one came in, so we just drank our beer in Cicero, rattling on about how light and easy it is to write some kind of a story, or novel . . . Then the writer told me in a whisper . . . Dad's a write-off, you know, a goner, he chain-smokes and he's diabetic . . . So, Dubenka, I duly got to know the Chicago suburb of Cicero and how its residents spend their Sunday afternoons . . .

Back home in Kersko on the 17th November I stood and looked up at the blue night sky — the moon rose, I was crowned with stars, my favourite constellation, Orion, shone out above the woods and over the neighbour's garden, and over my head the constellation of the Great Bear . . . I gave myself added courage, went home and put on the TV, our own TV, *Current Affairs*, and here it was at last . . . Here was the student procession led by Vasil Mohorita, marching solemnly along the designated candle-lit route from the dissecting lab, the same way Jan Opletal's remains were carried fifty years ago, but this candle-lit procession walked to the Slavín cemetery, and there at the memorial tablet to the poet Karel Hynek Mácha official youth-leader Vasil Mohorita himself laid a candle along with several other students . . . The cameras showed us all this, and recorded the official student march on its way back, — but the decent students encountered a still greater procession, also students, but 'disruptive elements', the commentator said, and the two streams merged, the bad ones persuaded the decent ones, and they all set off together down Plavecká towards the centre of town . . . I listened, Dubenka, I saw all this, and I felt pleased, I said to myself, at last we've been shown pictures of not only the decent ones, but also the bad ones, and the commentator spoke without undue emphasis, without raising his voice, without preaching . . . And I went to bed feeling that finally something was really happening in Prague, with authorisation from the Local National Committee . . .

But, next morning a friend from Prague came to see me, and his eyes were bursting, he'd witnessed it himself for four hours, he'd counted fifty thousand people in that huge procession moving all the way from Plavecká to the National Theatre, fifty thousand was his own rough estimate, based on a flow of about four people per square metre . . . And later, after dusk, by the Smíchov wine cellar, he'd seen National Avenue, Národní třída, packed with young people, calling out slogans, all wide-eyed — then, at about eight o'clock, the Interior Ministry forces in white helmets had attacked out of Spálená — but the students staged a sit-down, and there they were, face to face, the demonstrating students and young people sitting on the ground, holding up flowers and burning candles and singing . . . Then came a long moment of silence, followed by a clash and confusion, cries and shouting, and lamentation and screaming . . . And this friend of mine, who came to tell me this, his face was all pale and his eyes were staring, he said he'd never experienced the like — then he was separated from the others by the armed forces, who pushed him down to the pub U Medvídků, knocking over a few journalists . . . When he returned an hour later to the spot where the clash had come for those sitting and offering their little candles and flowers to the armed forces, there he saw — my friend said, wiping his wet face with his palm — he saw, lying on the asphalt and the pavement by the Reduta building, scarves and caps, a woman's bra even . . . and out of the arches an elderly man came weeping, holding a black shoe in one hand and a yellow shoe in the other . . . and the sound of singing, shouting and angry calls came from the National Theatre . . .

And what he saw, that friend of mine will never forget — though he'd seen many similar things and events before . . . And he saw later how groups of young people, the bolder ones, under the arches, over by the law office, and down Mikulandská and Voršilská, the bolder ones came, and there on the pavement under those several arcadings they laid candles at the spots still spattered with the warm blood of those who were beaten up . . .

And I thought in that moment, Dubenka, of Franz Kafka's childhood "Ouragan de décembre", those nationalist street fights and conflicts with the police, those anti-Semitic incidents, when the Vienna government declared a state of emergency in Prague — on that Saturday morning when my friend told me about what he'd seen, I also thought of burned-out Detroit, that centre of an industrial city, where black policemen did not and could not prevent the demonstrating people from getting what they wanted, for finally THE PEOPLE, yes, THE PEOPLE is the determining force that finally sweeps away everything that stands in its path . . . Yes, THE PEOPLE, even if they were just hundreds of thousands of young unarmed people, girls with unblinking eyes, thrilled to be walking through those Prague streets as if to their first dance, students and workers, pupils in tertiary education, apprentices in industrial training centres, the elderly and the old, who put aside their sobs and their tears, and even though they had meant to go elsewhere, walked along with the young ones . . . Yes, yes, this is THE PEOPLE of Carl Sandburg . . . and they went along with the youth, just like those demonstrations I saw in January and in October . . . And I'm sitting out here in Kersko watching yesterday's TV and sniffling at Vasil Mohorita leading the cortège authorised by the Local National Committee, the candle-lit cortège across Prague, from the mortuary to Slavín cemetery, to place a permitted candle on the tomb of Karel Hynek Mácha . . .

Dubenka, I meant to write about my American trip, but I'm endlessly excited by all of this, as recounted to me by people coming out of Prague. Please, I'll tell you about my trip round the universities another time, at the moment my spirit's in these universities of young life that stepped out again this Sunday and gathered again in Wenceslas Square and the adjoining streets . . . This time I saw the young people with my own eyes, the theatres were out on strike — and if John Reed had still been alive to see this city, he'd surely have written another *Eight Days* that shook not just Prague, but Central Europe too . . . Mr Dubček came out on this Prague afternoon to join those fifty thousand too, accompanied by a lady and a gentleman from the Italian press — Dubček caused no breach of the peace, but they ran him in, Dubenka, and released him three hours later — he was just happy to see the day when these young, different young people from twenty years ago, declared their trust in him by their actions . . .

And Dubenka, that evening I was in the Myrtle, when Pepča Čečil came along and said the bar-manager had given him permission to play the helicon, his bass tuba . . . just one wee song that Hašek used to sing back in the days of the old Austria. I listened as always . . . and Pepča sang that wee song, which I'm rather fond of, though it frightens me . . . "A Bomb Dropped on the Russians" . . . And the customers clapped, the bar-manager had unfortunately allowed only one song, but that was enough . . . "A Bomb Dropped on the Russians" . . . So that was the Sunday afternoon, and that was the Sunday evening! Which brings me to the subject of Chicago after all, for there in the Art Institute a gigantic picture hangs, more powerful than that song of "A Bomb Dropped on the Russians" . . . It's called *Sunday Afternoon on the Isle of la Grande Jatte*, and it measures 2½ by 3½ metres . . . But that's not why I'm telling you about Monsieur Seurat's picture — he was only just over thirty when he died . . . but his heart was greater than the Ritz Diamond, for it was he that said — to himself but not only to himself, to all young people, as if all the way here to Prague — that only a diamond can make a groove in another diamond . . .

Dear Dubenka, I meant to write to you about Ithaca, that was my plan, but this Monday in Prague is stronger than myself . . .

I went back to Kersko to feed the kitties, nearly all of them greet me, expecting me to bring them something to eat — as I step off the bus and walk over to my white striped gate and fence, they rush through the gaps and fly joyfully to meet me, even the rusty streaked old tabby cats turn somersaults, they trot along, and after them bounds Cassius Clay, who knows he's the one I carry in my hand, the one I nuzzle, burying my face in his shaggy fur, and asking him to stand by me, let nothing happen to me, so that I can go on writing to you in San Francisco, telling you these things which I rattle out of the typewriter into the pages of these letters — only Cassius knows, I whisper it to him, that I love you — it was for your sake that I shouted to Susanna on the way from Detroit to Chicago, I shouted to her, Is that thing loaded? And her camera was at the ready . . . the express stopped at that station carrying the name board saying Kalamazoo — Kalamazoo . . . so Susanna's camera caught me that Kalamazoo, the beautiful poem by Carl Sandburg, and Mister Hrabal's marvellous encounter with Carl Sandburg in Kalamazoo . . . The poem's called 'The Sins of

Kalamazoo' — when did I first read it? Forty, no, thirty years ago . . . and there's a passage in it . . . where lovers go to the post-office counter in Kalamazoo, and they say their names, asking after letters. And they say it again: "Is there really nothing for me? Please look again, there must be a letter for me . . ." But you don't expect one from me, since I don't send these letters, I only talk about them first with Cassius Clay, my little blackamoor — then my friends and I copy out these letters addressed to you, but actually to others too, let all who read get inky fingers with these letters of mine, these texts . . .

As I said, when I get to Kersko, all the kitties come to meet me, turning somersaults — and now I'm all *wetterkrank* with these cats of mine, *wetterkrank* with you too — *wetterkrank* because, if I write what I want to write, I write something I would rather whisper softly in your ear, like I used to whisper things to Mrs Pearl, my Pearl of Assurance . . . And now I go back to Prague, it's Monday, and there it is, I'm sniffling — I see it, I see this beauty of Prague, these lovely girls, these young men, students, stepping out all proud and solemn about how fate is not passing them by, but moving with them and through them — how they alone can make that groove in the diamond of our society, like diamonds they cut a diagonal across the Old Town Square, and pour down the Royal Route — I go to meet them, staring at the ground to hide the fact that I'm all weepy, I'm on the point of tears, for wherever I look, I see these unblinking eyes, eyes sharpened by a sense of where they're going and why, going not with knowledge, but with a leap, overleaping by their existence here and now in Prague all the knowledge, all the universities and polytechnics of the world, overleaping even the Castle itself, which is gloomy now, like when Rudolf of Habsburg lived there. I stop outside the Arts Faculty building on Celetná and read that the Faculty of Education is out on strike, there are newspaper cuttings, and fiery emphatic appeals to all who take the side of the young, who do not stand by on the pavement . . . And Dubenka, I am glad to have lived to see the sight of all this — just as we wept, Mr Mucha and I, to see that exhibition of modern, young, committed art in the old Holešovice slaughterhouse, we wept to have lived to see what we had no longer hoped for — the fault in the diamond, that sparkle, which is there still, shining out, immediately obvious . . . They come towards me, Dubenka, fine well-dressed young people — girls in their best make-up . . . as if they were on their way to a big party, a friend's wedding — but these girls are a wedding in themselves, they have wedded themselves to a joyous, human infinitude, in them the essential is conceived and made manifest, in them the dictate of being is made manifest, and I see that those who used to wander aimlessly about the city are full of dignity now — like back in the days when Sasha Dubček dived from the board in the swimming pool, and old ladies unhooked jewels and earrings and laid them at the altar of that young man, as he then was — who joined this afternoon's demonstrations in Prague . . . And the young men who cause trouble at football grounds, supporters of Sparta, Slavia or Bohemians, they were here too, stepping solemnly along as if it was their wedding day, the day they go to marry the girl they love . . . Through Staromák, the Old Town Square, the throngs pass, in their diagonals, horizontals and zig-zags — then on to Wenceslas Square, where ever since midday youths have been sitting at the hooves of

St. Wenceslas, and the police are behaving as if this time the Local National Committee for Prague 1 had agreed, and Comrade Štěpán had issued specific orders, that the police force should supervise this solemn Easter Monday, without the customary Easter thrashing . . .

And I go where I go, because, as you know, Dubenka, I'm on my own, I'm alone, I live on the street or go to Kersko and only return to my flat in Sokolníky to sleep . . . I know, I do have children, all the ones I've ever met, as well as all those who walk the streets and pavements — who know my heart's with them, but I have to watch myself a bit, because I'm old, and my heart's practically fit to burst with all this emotion, even if it's not as big as Andy Warhol's heart, a heart as big as the Ritz . . . which burst nevertheless! One banal operation on the gall bladder, and pop she goes! So I sit in the Tiger instead, drinking beer and signing my *Three Novellas*, just published during these Eight Days that Shook the City of Prague . . . And with me sits my friend Motýlek, who knows how to smile and dress so well — who's building the Prague Metro — who knows when not to talk, but now he tells me, Mr Hrabal, a girl came up in an unbuttoned shirt, saying she's here on behalf of the University Strike Committee, they want you to go to a theatre, to take part in a debate or something . . . He told me this, my friend Motýlek — who models himself on Steve McQueen — he gave a secret smile, then we said nothing, just looked at each other, then Jarda came over, a reader of mine — he's also building the Metro — and he said, Wenceslas Square's chock a block, right up to the horse's hooves . . . And we carried on drinking, but I was shaking all over, because writing letters to Dubenka — that

I could do, but what could I say to the young people, being about four generations older, and then . . . what about my Slav propensity to tears — I know, Dubenka, the heroes of Dostoyevsky novels also like to weep a lot, with their mild cholera, induced by the drink . . . actually I've got mild cholera too, just like Dostoyevsky did . . . And now it happened, down the main aisle between the tables and chairs came the girl mentioned by Motýlek — called this by his friends after the film and hero of that name — it's Czech for butterfly, Papillon — and Motýlek fingered his earlobe, tattooed with a *papillon*, a tiny butterfly . . . This Marseillaise girl came along in her unbuttoned shirt and her jeans, a mug of beer in one hand, and a cigarette in the other, she sat down and she said . . . Mr Hrabal, in the name of the Strike Committee, I invite you to come along with me, we're having a debate — you won't turn us down, will you? Just come along with me . . . I said to her . . . Yes, that's all very well, dear, but I've been laid up with a heart condition . . . What if I went and collapsed? Then two more students came up, lads the size of Motýlek . . . and I said . . . Come on, here's two of my *Letters to Dubenka*, 'The White Horse' and 'Greyhound Story' . . . Take a look, you Marseillaise girl! It's all about what's been happening, not just what you've been living through in Prague, but it's a love story too . . . The girl with the free-flowing hair was really emphatic, theatrical, as was and is the custom at such moments . . . she looked at the text . . . and she smiled, rejoicingly, put her empty glass down right on one of my letters to you, Dubenka, and said . . . Can we use it? . . . Said I: You may . . . So the University Strike Committee left, it made its theatrical exit . . . And there I sat there feeling a bit sorry for myself — I'd brought along some Spanish olives, so I started on them, and Mr Díp brought me some sausage and black pudding in a bag, whispering . . . Eat it yourself when you get home! Then he offered me a bakelite bowl of aspic as well . . . while Mr Václav brought a paper bag of crescent rolls . . . We ate slowly, then Motýlek glanced at his watch and said . . . Christ, I've got to go, we're having suckingpig . . . And we sat on, and folks talked to me, but I was deaf to the world, the University Strike Committee had really got me down . . . Mr Anderle turned up with his wife Milada, they smiled at me, Milada stroked the back of my hand, then spotting all the strokes on my beer mat, she said: Bohoušku, you mustn't drink like that . . . Meanwhile Mr Anderle enlightened me about everything I knew already — looking at his watch anxiously and saying he had to get home, so as not to miss any of the events on TV . . . So I left with my friends the Anderles . . . Outside there was a roaring din, the thunderous roar came nearer, as the giant throng returned over the bridges from the Castle — but armed men in white helmets barred the way . . . and against the flood, like swollen rivers, the gigantic throng surged backward . . . And I excused myself, saying that I had to see some friends at the pub U knihovny, someone was expecting me — a man to whom I always owe a great debt for a few words of fortification, though really he needs fortifying the most . . . But he wasn't there, I walked through the close defile of drinkers — here and there the foam of their beer brushed against my little blue rucksack, bought me by Stephanie, that student of Czech, Dubenka, in your native city of Lincoln, Nebraska . . . And out I went with my blue, damp rucksack, and my Russian sable fur cap, bought in Moscow, which suits me like the one Andy Warhol himself wore in the snow-clad mountains . . . That winter when I was in Moscow I popped into the big department store GUM, and hey, there stood a Russian, on his head a sable fur cap, to which I took a fancy, so I said: How much? and there in that stream of people he put it on me — it fitted — so I said again: How much? and he indicated three hundred and fifty . . . so I drew out three hundred roubles . . . and he shrugged his shoulders and removed the cap from my head . . . and I drew out fifty marks . . . I showed him this fifty marks, he inspected the banknote expertly, and kept it, planting the sable fur hat back on my head, — straightaway the woman with him pulled another identical cap out of her bag, and this theatrical, manly Russian, who looked like Andy Warhol, stuck it on his head, leaned back against the corner of GUM — people streamed by — and there he stood, arms folded and one tall boot creased at the knee, he stood there, and he knew that any moment now somebody else would come up to him, someone just like me . . . So there I stood in front of the pub in my Russian fur hat, while all the people who'd been in Wenceslas Square streamed past me, shouting and carrying placards — I watched them, astonished at this May Day parade on Easter Monday, still without its customary whippings and lashings . . . I'd never seen so many beautiful unblinking people, I'd never seen such solemnity in young people . . . I walked along with them, and I came to my old Law Faculty, where across the bridge the white helmets gleamed and shone, proclaiming no entry — and I stood where fifty years ago I saw the Army and SS-Waffe hounding my fellow-students out of the Faculty — it was morning, my friends from the University were forced at rifle butt into army trucks with green tarpaulins, while I stood on the corner of Bílkova and saw what I saw ... And as the side-flaps were slammed shut, and those lorries set off, making for Sachsenhausen, I heard my fellow-students singing ... *Kde domov můj* ... our national anthem ... Today I stood there and saw young men in jeans bending their knees and squatting down on a patch of lawn to light candles by a little memorial I'd never spotted before ... three young lads squatting there in jeans, anoraks, scarves and waistcoats, as if they were warming their hands, their heads just above the flames of the thin candles ... And I heard the tram coming, my number seventeen, so I rushed the short distance to the stop and caught it, Dubenka, and went off home ... And I couldn't help it, Dubenka, the next morning, I took the number seventeen back, I stepped on to the lawn, there was the marble tablet, and I ran my fingers over what was written there ... "In memory of an unknown fighter, who fell in the service of freedom, May 1945."

P.S.

Dear Dubenka, I've read so many catchwords and slogans ... But to you, teaching Russian at that University of yours in the afternoons and making a living at the department store in the mornings, to Stanford University in California, I send the only slogan I remembered that Monday ...

ALL PRAGUE TODAY
TOMORROW THE WHOLE COUNTRY

21 November 1989

Meshuge Stunde

Dubenka,

I feel it's my duty, when I read something that moves me, to put it in my letters to you. Mr Rüdiger Safranski states in the Preface to his book *Schopenhauer und Die wilden Jahren der Philosophie* that at the end, towards the end of his life, Schopenhauer said, "A philosophy where you do not hear between the pages the tears, the wailing and gnashing of teeth, and the fearful tumult of general mutual murder, is no philosophy." And, Safranski continues, "In a view of the French revolution, Kant, midwife of the 'wild years of philosophy', had written: 'Such a phenomenon in man's history can never be forgotten, for it has disclosed an aptitude and a power within human nature for the better . . .' " Mr Safranski observes, "Our events, those which we can never forget, are called Auschwitz, the Gulag Archipelago and Hiroshima." . . . Die wilden Jahren: Kant, Fichte, Hegel, junge Marx . . .

I spoke with a man who lived through those terrible events in Romania, in Bucharest. The children who were shot, those barefoot kneeling children in Timișoara, he saw all that. But appalling too was the drained blue swimming pool into which they cast the living soldiers of Ceaușescu's Commando, as the Father of the Nation termed them . . . Ceaușescu's children. Those children, swarming and alive, condemned to death, because of their upbringing.

Dubenka, it was a long time ago, but memory makes the past into a new present, so listen to this story of how once, maybe half, or a quarter of a century ago, the famous conductor Leopold Stokowski stayed at the Golden Goose, the Hotel Šroubek, on Prague's Wenceslas Square. He'd been conducting the Czech Philharmonic . . . and when the time came for him to get a taxi from the hotel to the station, however hard the porters tried, no taxi arrived, there was no sign of a taxi. And the Paris express will not wait . . . So there Stokowski stood with his five or more suitcases and bags . . . when who should come along in a little trolley but a young man, who sized up the situation immediately, addressed the Maestro in fluent English and offered him a lift . . . So they all got onto the trolley, not only the luggage, but Leopold Stokowski too, a fine, handsome, elegantly dressed man . . . and slowly but surely the trolley conveyed the lot of them to the railway station . . . Leopold Stokowski, who performed in that film *One Hundred Men and a Girl*. And, Dubenka, who else do you think played in that film . . . That little girl star Shirley Temple . . . Who today has an article in our daily newspaper *Free Word* . . .

In August 1968, by some ironic quirk of fate, I was in Prague as a delegate of the World Health Organisation, and I witnessed your revolution. Last year I returned to your country, coincidentally it was August again, and I was able to follow, not only the actual events of your Velvet Revolution . . . but also the period preceding it . . . Your people looked subdued, subjugated even. Their eyes in the metro looked down and avoided each others' gaze. At the same time, however, their eyes radiated a longing to communicate, to say something . . . I took part as a private individual in the 28th October demonstration on Wenceslas

Square. My sports outfit and training shoes helped me run the gauntlet of the police barriers, as I joined the young people in fleeing from the forces of law and order . . . This, Dubenka, is the account of Mrs Shirley Temple, child heroine of that film with Leopold Stokowski *One Hundred Men and a Girl*. And she goes on: *I deny the allegation made at the time by the newspaper* Rudé Právo, *claiming I used a room at the Hotel Yalta with a fine view of the statue of Wenceslas as a kind of observation post . . . I particularly admire the decent manner in which the Velvet Revolution was conducted, and the courage and pride of your young people . . . I was saddened by the brutal intervention of the security forces on National Avenue. American journalists were amongst those seriously wounded . . .* Dubenka, it makes a marvellous collage: the memory of the heroine of that film *One Hundred Men and a Girl . . .* alongside that image of the grown-up woman, Ambassador of the Delighted States in Prague . . .

Dubenka, now please stand by me, I call upon you, please stand by me . . . I've just seen again on television the abdication of the President of our unfortunate Republic, the abdication of Husák, he tiptoed away from the presidential throne as if nothing had happened, as if he had just announced the current meteorological situation, he tiptoed away from what he himself had cooked up as head of state, he went like a blind old fox . . . Now I'd like to quit the world the way that Romanian Count Dracula did, that Maldoror, that loftiest simulacrum of evil . . . but I know what I'm really like . . . in the end I'll slink off all the same, like an old, a blind old fox . . .

Dubenka, Mr Safranski ends his Preface to Schopenhauer's biography as follows: "The wild years of philosophy ignored this philosopher of the 'wailing and gnashing of teeth' and the age-old art of the contemplative life which desires to achieve Peace and Calm. The wild years ignored this philosopher who, far ahead of his time, had apprehended the three great afflictions of human megalomania. The cosmological affliction: Our world is one of numberless spheres in endless space, on which a mouldy coating of living and cognitive beings vegetates. The biological affliction: Man is an animal, in whom intelligence must compensate for lack of instincts and poor organic adaptation to life. The psychological affliction: Our conscious I is not master in its own house. These are the three great afflictions of human megalomania . . ."

But Dubenka — now for something more cheerful! When I was in Sofia some years ago, there in front of my hotel stood the man it was named after. Stalin himself. The citizens were considerate, they said, with the onset of winter women came in the afternoons to dress Stalin in some warm long-johns and a nice warm shirt, and a fur cap with flaps, so that Stalin wouldn't catch cold here in Bulgaria. Dubenka, would that such a tradition might still be kept up, such a fine custom that was . . . In the same way, James Joyce sadly tells in his *Ulysses* of Mr Leopold Bloom remembering the coffin his little son Rudy lay in, and how his mother, Mrs Marion Bloom, had knitted him a long warm jersey, so that her little son wouldn't get cold in the grave.

Dear Dubenka, if in the Bulgarian capital, when the weather turns cold, the little women come at dusk and dress Stalin in warm clothing, here in Prague, you know, the same thing used to be done in ages past, every day they used to dress up the little figure of the Bambino di Praga, nuns even came down, from the Roudnice nunnery, I think, and every day the Bambino di Praga would be dressed up in different clothes — the most precious child mannequin on earth . . . And so, as I've written elsewhere, and as I heard from the Lady Ambassador, General Klecanda's wife — over in Bolivia the Indians wear medallions with the image of this Infant Jesus of Prague, and among the Indians legend has it that Prague must be the loveliest city in the world, because, according to the Indians, Prague was where the Infant Jesus went to school . . . Princess Lobkovitz built the Bambino's church, and her family after her kept up the trust, so that each and every day Prague's Infant Jesus could wear different clothes from the day before, and so it went on, the whole year round: three hundred and sixty-five complete sets of clothes, embroidered and stitched by the nimble fingers of the nuns and their helpers . . .

But now you ask me, Dubenka, how am I going to connect the Velvet Revolution with all this stuff about the Bambino di Praga? But Dubenka, can't you see the connection? The South American Indians have this legend that Prague is the loveliest city in the world. Why? Because little Jesus went to school there. And who made the Velvet Revolution? Millions of little Jesuses, dressed up as students, actors, clowns and young people, who gave precedence over strict knowledge to the inclinations of their heart . . . General Šalgovič, however, the man who supervised the landing of heavy Soviet aircraft at Ruzyně airport in 1968, he hanged himself yesterday in the laundry . . . Of course there are some spots which can't be washed out without damaging the nature of the fabric . . .

My dear Dubenka, I took the number twelve tram up to town to pay my respects to Prague's Infant Jesus, to the Bambino di

Praga . . . But how I overestimated myself! I had to get off that number twelve in a hurry and rush down to the public lavatories . . . But I knocked in vain . . . They were open, but all the lavatories were engaged. I begged the loo attendant . . . For Jesus' sake, get me a cubicle! But the old lady with Sibylline eyes merely gave a wave of the hand . . . All occupied . . . By the time a lavatory compartment finally became free, I had to confess what had happened. And the loo lady said . . . Not to worry, sir, it's hardly the first time, something of the sort happens here practically every day . . . specially if there's a big holiday or some large gathering . . . The real disaster comes when you get a rally or a congress, or mass tours to view the beauties of Prague . . . That lady gazed at me, she had lovely eyes, just like the cloakroom lady who narrates the story of 'Buchmendel', by the tragic Stefan Zweig . . . What am I to do? I said . . . Take off your dirty underpants, and look here. See? I've got a little tub and a basin, and I've even got a washboard . . . You can rinse out your underpants here, and here's a hair-dryer . . . Or you can pop them on the line . . . Once I even got told off by the cops, when the Spartakiáda was on, for hanging out ladies' knickers in the arches opposite the Malá Strana Café . . . And so, disgustedly, first I took bog roll, then I washed and scrubbed, the water ran, and I washed and scrubbed, while customers came and went, and the attendant sat heavily on her chair, she rested her hands on her knees and she told me all about it . . . Even had the aristocracy in here, caught short the same as you . . . A Spanish countess for instance . . . just like you, washing and scrubbing away on the washboard with her frilly purple pantaloons . . . Now if only I could write . . . And there I washed and I scrubbed, and it felt like

something out of Dante's *La Divina Commedia*: Purification —
Purgatory . . . And the loo lady sat there and carried on talking . . .
Know what happened one day? This tram driver came rushing in,
just like you — but he'd hardly done his business and paid and gone
back upstairs, when he was straight back again . . . And so it went
on, he was up and down about ten times . . . There at the stop his
tram stood, jingling away . . . He'd come over all pale by now. He
told me he was on the number twenty-two . . . It had come on sudden like, mid-route, so he just slammed on the brake and ran
straight down . . . In half an hour the effect was catastrophic — the
inspector came rushing in, because that tram of his was blocking
all the others practically the whole way back to the National
Theatre . . . So the inspector decided he'd have to take the tram
himself . . . By this time the man was pale, sir, beyond recognition,
you could tell he'd shat his guts out . . . Pity I don't know how to
write . . . He and I we had a grand old chat, and there he was, just
like you, washing out his long-johns in the tub, rubbing them on
the washboard. He wore them really long, down to his ankles, on
strings . . . Just like Franta Hrubín, the poet, you know, 'National
Artist' — who also washed his long-johns out here once and went
on about what a lovely experience it was . . . How it sort of opened
up for him a truer insight into the human race . . . And here's the
jug if you like, he says . . . And off I hop to U Schnellů to get
Hrubín his jug of beer . . .

But I still haven't told you, Dubenka, about our tomcats and
their *meshuge Stunden*. Once a day, all of a sudden, my cats are
seized by an hour of crazy behaviour, out of the blue they go totally
nuts and start flying about all over the cottage garden, acting as if

they've gone off their rockets, everything for them is suddenly alive and living, under every little leaf they find mice, and they paw away as if they were seeking and finding ping-pong balls. Then suddenly they speed off again at a gallop, in their headlong rush they gash each other's ears with their paws and their claws, they leap on each other, roll over, then the three gangs of them declare an open revolution, an uprising, hissing and mewing resounds all over the lot, out of the blue they rush out swiftly at those spruces and stubby little oaks and fight together up there in the tree-tops, and then they let themselves down again on their hind legs, they come slowly down, but some of the toms stay up in the branches, and while those below fight and hiss at each other, those up above flash their eyes at one another and fight on like that, until they too lower themselves down the branches to the ground, or even fall, but that doesn't stop them — my three gangs carry on playing up like this, flying along the path beside the fence, rushing through the lattices, tearing their ears and flying off again somewhere over by the stream, then they turn and speed back again, one after another, at a gallop, with powerful great leaps they fly back under my windows — and if I'm brave enough, I go out and look at this cats' *meshuge Stunde*, and find that almost all the tomcats have purposely gone nuts, panting away with their little tongues sticking out, harum scarum wide-eyed, haring around those great pines and oaks, in opposite directions, only to collide and claw one another with a terrific yowl, truss themselves up into a ball, tear at one another's ears mercilessly and repeatedly . . . Those long leaps, a sudden mad dart up branches and trunks, along branches onto twigs, and then lowering themselves down again to the ground —

but even when they're still in mid-air, before landing, they fight, they pretend to fight . . . Sometimes I'm glad when, during this cats' *meshuge Stunde*, the Soviet planes come past, flying low over the woods — Milovice isn't far from here, with its Soviet planes which take off and land making a frightful racket and din . . . It affects my cats too . . . Even in the middle of their *meshuge Stunde* . . . those aeroplanes horrify them so — they fall, pressing their little bellies into the leaves and moss, totally flattening themselves with horror . . . Some of the tomcats fly up to their nooks among the coal and in the wood pile and don't creep out till the Soviet aircraft have landed over there beyond the woods, on the Milovice airfield . . . They happen once a day, my cats' *meshuge Stunden*, then they get their breath back, it takes them a long time to calm down, slow down . . . These, writes Safranski, are the *meshuge Jahren der Philosophie* . . . Kant, Fichte, Hegel, and the young Marx . . . But now it's evening, in three days we'll have a full moon. It's got to me too, for three days I've had the flu, and fevers, which have subsided now, I'm able to go out and look at the evening — I feel restless, the moon's been out a long time, now it climbs sharply up over the wood and the garden in front of the cottage, now it's almost as if the moon too were having its own *meshuge Stunde*, it climbs so swiftly heavenward, I sit at my window, and the moon is so high in the sky I have to turn and twist my head to get a view of it, I sit here for a bit and get the feeling that my house, thanks to its windows, is just like a great big cut diamond, and I know where my cats are now . . . I can see glimpses of them through the window, beside the white fence, around the beige track, so I go out after them and sure enough, the kits are sitting over there by the white laths, just like at midday, when the sunlight warms them and they bake themselves there in the grass . . . but now they sit there solemnly, erect, leaning their backs against the latticed laths and squinting up at the sky, where the moon is shining, and they are listening, tuning in to that silence just like me . . . I walk past them like a President filing out his Castle guard, the kits follow after me, the procession closes up, they escort me wherever I go . . . In the day I get scared of the gamekeepers seeing us, me and my twelve cats following along behind me, dancing and leaping about, lying joyously on their backs and twirling in the sand and smiling, even now in the moonlit night they smile, because they are happy that I'm alive on this earth . . . And as always Cassius Clay comes along, the little black tom — he rises up on his hind legs, and I have to catch hold of him, and lift him up straightaway, and press his fur, his furry tummy to my face . . . That's our ceremony, none of the other cats is brave enough . . . They'd all like to be picked up too, but they don't dare, they only show by all their dancing about just within shooting range that they would like to do it too, but they don't have the courage . . . Maybe it's enough for them that Blacking, as I sometimes call Cassius, does it for them . . . And I close my eyes, and the fur sizzles out his scent, and Cassius probably knows, because all day he does nothing but clean himself, clean himself all over, just in case I happen to come and pick him up in my hand and press my face into his fur and speak tender words, like the ones I have said maybe only to You, Dubenka, and then only in spirit, but Cassius knows that I really do speak to him, he closes his eyes, his fuses go, and for a moment he looks quite dead . . . Sometimes the sooty orphan from my sister-in-law's comes, the one left from that pair who always trotted out together to meet me, pulling on invisible threads after them a little invisible, but so needful truckload of happiness. Sometimes I go to find him, I know where he is, he sits near the gate and waits, just in case the one who died in front of the locked door to the house, his kid brother, turns up today . . . And he came along in the moonlit night, I picked him up in my hand, but it wasn't a comfort to him that day, he rattled, he's probably got pneumonia . . . And, Dubenka, he's altogether neglected, like I was when my Pipsi died. I clean him with a rag, I clean his ears, I take him to the others to please him, but he only stays on for a little while, as I walk through the moonlit night he trots along behind me for a bit, then goes back again, he can't settle, he's aged terribly, this tender little tom who always used to look after himself like Cassius. Maybe he'll get over it. Today he comes as usual, mewing softly at the latticing, glancing under my sister-in-law's caravan, standing in front of the locked door, then he lies down under the round table where the newspapers and magazines are kept . . . And then he can't help it, he goes off to keep watch, just in case his sooty little brother turns up. So he stands there in the meadow, looking around, waiting, he stands where he can be seen, but it's no use, it would take a miracle, but there are no miracles any more, nor is there living water . . . His little brother is buried out there, behind the big oak tree where they both used to like lying out in the sunshine, by the roots of the mighty oak . . .

So, Dubenka, that's how it ends. The happiness of those two did not last for long, but it was worth it. Just as we have really seen so little of each other here on this earth, and look, I am the same as if you were beside me. These invisible threads, these invisible threads, these invisible threads? But where would we be, without these invisible threads . . . Who will bring me three mustard grains from a house where no-one has died? So there is nothing for it but Te Deum laudamus.

P.S.

Dear Dubenka, Arthur Schopenhauer's mother Johanna got her son to write a diary when he was young. Please let me translate a small entry for you — made when he was twelve: "Wednesday 16th June. Towards midday we departed from Hamburg and after several hours of gloomy weather we reached the Zollenspieker ferry, where we were to be taken across the Elbe. Then before the ferry-boat arrived, we started talking to a poor blind lady, who had no idea when it was day and when it was night. When we asked her the reason for her blindness, she told us, that during the half-hour journey in the frost to her christening, her eyes had got frostbitten . . . Yet although she'd been blind ever since, she knew all the roads, and everything she needed she could take care of by herself. I felt sorry for this woman, I wondered at the phlegmatic calm with which she bore her suffering. She had paid so dearly for the consolation of becoming a Christian woman! From the Zollenspieker ferry we went on our way after a filling lunch and in the evening we reached Lüneburg, where I saw nothing but Gothic buildings . . ."

Of course! Dear Dubenka . . . the 150,000 copies of my book *November Hurricane*, are held up for 'technical reasons', until March, or maybe, dear April, until April. T. S. Eliot . . . "April is the cruellest month . . .", *The Waste Land*, "breeding Lilacs out of the dead land . . ."

CORRIGENDUM

In this letter it was not only the cats who were *meshuge*, so was I! I was quite convinced that the girl in the film *One Hundred Men and a Girl* was Shirley Temple, our present American Ambassador . . . but one of my readers, Mrs Eva Janovcová, has written me a lovely letter telling me to let her beloved Durbin be, for the part of the girl in *One Hundred Men and a Girl* was played by Deanna Durbin . . . So I apologise to all my readers and most of all to Mrs Janovcová . . . Of course! To me this fiction is all the dearer, for being less truthful, and hence more beautiful.

A Pity We Didn't Burn
to Death Instead
(Anglo-Epidiascope)

Dear Dubenka,

I like to think of myself as a bit of an enlightener. Take for instance
the answer to the question, where does Eastern Europe really
begin? For the Sudeten Germans the Balkans began in North
Bohemia, just past Lovosice. Don't be shocked by this — maps
compiled by the ancient Romans identify the Sudetens as a terri-
tory consisting of the same belt of mountains and hills as today.
For me, on the other hand, Eastern Europe used to begin where
the Empire-style Austrian railway stations ended. However! For
the artists of the Café Slavia Eastern Europe began in the Karlín
district of Prague. The composer Rychlík obstinately insisted that
Eastern Europe began just beyond Prague's Poříčí Gate. And now,
just imagine what happened to me. I was invited to Glasgow
University, to its Czech department . . . Throughout the whole
Anglo-Saxon world Czech is a part of Russian studies, — and
what's more, I was their guest on that very afternoon when
Glasgow Russian Studies was celebrating the fiftieth, or was it the
fifty-first anniversary of its foundation, and there was a party, with
champagne, and the *pièce de résistance* of the whole occasion was a
giant oblong gateau about fifty centimetres by thirty-five. It stood

in the centre of the Russian lecture hall, it was iced with a thick layer of beige sugary stuff, and on top of it, at the request of the head of department, there was a Jackson Pollock style gestural map, which showed not only Russia with the Urals and a red Soviet flag, but also Poland and Czechoslovakia with Polish and Czechoslovakian flags . . . and the head of the Czech section, Igor Hájek, entrusted me with the honourable task of cutting this cake with an enormous knife, and there I stood like Prince Metternich after the Napoleonic Wars, or like Stalin and Churchill over the map of the globe at the end of the Second World War . . . and all those present gathered round me so that everyone could get a view of this cake-cutting, for these Czechs have also acquired the Scottish sweet tooth . . . and everyone waited for their slice . . . but I stood there with the knife, I leaned over that giant cake and I smiled . . . if only Moscow could have seen this, Dubenka, if only Gorbachev could have seen me neatly placing the knife and carving up the Soviet Union right across the Urals, the sugar flag of the Soviet Union was blocking my way even, so I just sliced it in half with a mighty scrunch. After that the rest was easy, cutting half in half and so on, till I'd cut the thing up into slices the size of our old punch cake . . . each took a slice, and teachers and students alike recognised the onerous burden I had taken upon myself, at first I felt a sense of fright, but then I said to myself . . . What can they do to me anyway? And the teachers and students applauded as I completed my partition of the sugary map of Europe, this *Itio in partes*, I exclaimed, savouring with body and soul my own Peace of Westphalia after the Thirty Years' War . . . *cuius regio, eius religio . . .*

Dubenka, so I'm a bit of an educator and an enlightener, you see, and you're a student and teacher at Stanford University. Actually I'm my own enlightener, not only do I like imagining these scenes which I've tried to present you in this serial of epistles, I also like to entertain myself . . . To be educated, Dubenka, is a part of entertainment, and without enjoyment there's no point in education. So there. Furthermore, Dubenka . . . as Joseph Brodsky replied on the theme of East and West . . . if I were to trace an ideal boundary between East and West, between Europe and Asia, I wouldn't draw it at the Urals or even at the Soviet border, I'd put it along the course of the river Elbe. The journal *Express* notes how amazingly the words of the poet are now coming true, it's a bit like the demarcation line I drew with that sharp knife through the cake with its map of those territories where Russian, Czech, Slovak and Polish are spoken . . . a sharp cut, dividing and separating Asia and European Russia across the Urals . . . Dubenka, how distant is that idea of Sergey Yesenin . . . of Ru-ss-ia . . . O my Ru-ss-ia . . . Ra-see-ya ma-yaah . . . that Asiatic land! . . . How closely distanced are the ideas of the Sudeten German — that Eastern Europe begins just beyond Lovosice . . . and the composer Rychlík — that Eastern Europe starts, not even in Karlín, but just the other side of Prague's Poříčí Gate!

Dear Dubenka, I'm going to try and write you a few fresh memories of my English trip, acting on Roland Barthes' principle of . . . *lernen-verlernen, apprendre-désapprendre* . . . I didn't keep any notes, I merely apprehended what I saw . . . I can only write whatever has stuck in my mind, whatever has bobbed up to the surface . . . I began with me in Scotland, where I'd flown from London, I remember that afternoon at the University, after the anniversary party I had a discussion, or rather, the students of Czech and Slavonic put me various questions and I attempted to answer them, it was all over in an hour, then Mr Igor Hájek took me out for a drive in the car, I only remember the docks, the shipyard where the Queen Mary was built maybe half a century ago, the biggest liner in the world, we drove round that dock, now it's nothing but a huge ditch, for the Queen Mary was more than three hundred metres long . . . the original crane was still there, left as a memento, all brightly painted, I don't remember what colour, I only know it's a great giant, maybe eighty metres tall, like something dreamt up by the American sculptor Calder, it's monumental, this crane, like Prague's outlook tower on Petřín Hill, all the bits and pieces of that crane were quite functional, but to me that artefact seemed like a sombre solemn homage to Alexander Calder . . . Then they took me to an off-licence, the shop was like a prison inside, a wonderful jail, the shelves with their hundreds of different kinds of whisky and slender pistols of wine were all behind bars, speaking to the shopkeeper felt like visiting time at the jail, the Scots selected and paid for their purchases through the bars, and received their bottles gift-wrapped, again passed through the bars, hand to hand . . . Igor told me this was the general custom, similarly all over England taxis have a grille which separates the driver from passengers with a kind of holy-water aperture, a kind of open metal pocket, through which passengers first pay, and then receive their change, through this shiny, open palm of a pocket, it helps to eliminate trouble and misunderstanding . . . even prevents crime. That same evening we went to a Bohemian-style pub with various friends of Igor Hájek's, the place had scenes of Gypsy, Hungarian life round the walls, but most importantly, something that plagued me all over Britain, it was furiously cold, and when it's cold in a restaurant, the place goes miserable. Throughout my stay in Britain I had this yearning to get myself some warm Jaeger underwear, I even put my pyjamas on under my clothes, but I still felt cold, all the more when I remembered how I'd flown out of Prague in beautiful weather, almost hot it was, leaving at home all my various long-legged pants and warm sweaters, scarves and wrist-warmers, everything I should've taken with me, all of it left at home . . . And my hosts would be asking me what it was like during the Velvet Revolution, while I just felt miserably cold, maddened with all the chill, I even tried ordering a dish of pickled herring, rollmops, and drinking a tankload of beer, but it didn't help, I tried vodka too, Gorbatschow vodka . . . and that evening . . . I was the guest of Glasgow University, staying in one of their guest rooms . . . I collected the blankets off all the beds and tried to sleep, but really I just looked forward to going home and putting on all that warm underwear lying fallow there in my wardrobe, heaped up in piles . . . in that foretaste of wrapping myself up in all the warmth I'd left behind, I gave myself another dose of Belaspon, on top of that another dose of Rohypnol . . . and slowly, ever so slowly I dropped off, petrified of being woken by the cold!

On Sunday we set off north of Glasgow, the man from Czech studies Mr Čulík had said he'd give me a trip out to the lochs . . . and that was the real thing, it was cold like the High Tatras, or the top of Sněžka in the Krkonoše . . . but still the car was heated at least! You must go there sometime! If we were young, at least if I was, where best to take your honeymoon? In the Scottish lochs! I've never seen anything so lovely, such lovely villages, so many flowers, a million sheep and lambs, and those hills, suddenly I didn't even feel cold with all that beautiful countryside around me, I'm a great sheep fan, you know, and I'm a fan of rhododendrons, too, and those colours, it was as if they'd been seen and painted by Henri Matisse, those pastel shades! Rhododendrons of every hue, each one fresher than the last, and every cottage, even the poorest, full of flowers and a sense of decorative living, the meanest one-room dwelling was a real artefact! And those hills, planted by nature or by human hands with saturated-yellow clumps of gorse, *hlodáš* in the Czech, as Mr Čulík informed me, which sounds like "gnawing bush", and right enough, those yellow bushes gnawed away at my retinas, and my soul and spirit, if I have any . . . and those young lambs, obedient to their mums . . . when the road crossed into the estate of another owner, at the dividing line there was always a cattle grid of bars, rails set ever so slightly far apart . . . just calculated to break your leg . . . and what did I see? All my life I'd been teetering along like this! . . . The minute a lamb sensed with its hoof it might break its little leg, it backed off, it felt and it knew its limit . . . And I said: There's a million sheep here, Mr Čulík, what happens if it snows . . . He said: Well, what with the effect of the Gulf Stream, it only lasts a couple of days . . . I said: But what if there is a longer than usual snowfall? . . . In that case, Mr Čulík said, the shepherds and the sheep-farmers with their dogs have to go up into the hills and the mountains, and lift up the sheep to stop them from suffocating in the snowdrifts . . . for nights on end they roam about the slopes lifting and supporting and sheltering the sheep and their grown lambs . . . saving them . . . Christ in the Bible is always a shepherd to his flock . . .

So you see, Dubenka, this imaginary honeymoon of mine kept piling on the revs, higher and higher, I couldn't get enough of this feast for sore eyes . . . rough-hewn but beautiful flower-adorned villages, buildings, raw beautiful nature, festooned with rhododendrons and yellow explosions of furze . . . and as Mr Čulík told me, right up north, where the Gulf Stream curves around the coast, even palm trees grow . . . and I just stared at the blue interlocked lochs, green at the edges and nippy with the air that floats above the waters . . . and sheep toddled along the track, which now turned into an ordinary road, where our tyres rattled in the grit . . . and so after three hundred kilometres and more we reached a spot with a hotel, and right next to it a streaming and thundering waterfall, cars parked nearby, and guests readied themselves for lunch or walked along the shore of the cold blue and green loch, which mirrored a sky saturated with chillness and slantwise falling snow . . . I put on everything I had and still I was cold, I was carrying my green JANSPORT rucksack, the one a student of Czech bought for me, Dubenka, in that native city of yours . . . whose name escapes me, but I'll remember it, you'll see, in a future letter . . . but I was so cold, as I stood in front of that waterfall, that it felt palpably and precisely as though, instead of that JANSPORT rucksack on my back, the blue, chill, spray-adorned waterfall was just pouring down my spine . . . So we went inside, into the hotel . . . and a strange hotel it was too, full of well-off people, but worndown with age and melancholy and depression, and though they were all smartly and neatly attired, like shop-window dummies, the men kept checking to see if their shirt cuffs were tidy and their ties were neat and straight . . . and the women checked their dyed hair, and anxiously inspected their watches, so as not to miss their lunchtime, and crossed legs over knees . . . and the men looked in their pocket mirrors in case their ties were skew-whiff . . . and Mr Čulík and I had some of that aperitif honoured by poets . . . you see what a memory I have, Dubenka, the liqueur which Verlaine used to drink himself to death . . . and after that we had some stout, this time in honour of Dublin, and of Joyce, some Guinness, and then, to really warm ourselves up (the cold was soul-destroying . . . why why do we have this thing they call a spirit?), we took out the tape-recorder and recorded a great long interview . . . drinking that beer, that Dublin porter, Guinness, as it was drunk in Ormond's Bar by Stephen Dedalus' dad and his mates . . . Earlier on, in London, or in Birmingham, they told me the proper best Guinness was only to be had in Dublin, in the pubs next to the brewery, that's where the real devotees are, for barrels of Guinness can't tolerate long-distance transport . . . my photographer in London invited me to come to Dublin, to spend a whole week just drinking Guinness and visiting all the roads and streets and riverside quays of Dublin where Leopold Bloom and Stephen Dedalus went, Ulysses and his son Telemachus, and friends and all . . .

As we drove back to Glasgow, the road was just as resplendently bedecked as it was on our journey out to the lochs, only backwards. We went a different route, the country was even lovelier because we had time to indulge in it . . . Fifty kilometres out of Glasgow a giant factory loomed up, even larger than that travelling crane, a giant cube, cinnamon in colour, and then another. Here they distil whisky for the whole world, Ballantine's whisky . . . And so to the aeroplane, where I managed to warm up a little . . .

At the airport in London someone was meant to meet me, but we missed each other. It was freezing cold, and I caught a taxi. It was Sunday, streams of cars were returning from the weekend, and we drove at a snail's pace for two hours, but I was just glad to get properly warmed up at last in this taxi . . . In the middle of London I saw a woman leant against a plane tree being sick, a policeman was standing next to her, holding some sort of document, resting his hand gently on the sick lady's back. Asking about this, I was told that she must have been pregnant, the English have a reverential attitude to pregnant women, ladies in this blessed state even have the right to pee in the public square . . .

And again . . . At the hotel where I stayed my room was so cold . . . on top of that there was the constant noise of some kind of workshop or laundry, morn till night, all week long, till I had to plug up my ears with soft bread . . . I preferred to sit in the foyer, gazing out through the glass windows and walls on to the street, — I couldn't get enough of the garish double-decker buses. There I sat in my plush armchair, watching guests of all races and nationalities coming and going. The plush armchair warmed my back, and the black girl bartender warmed me up with sugary glances, for the day I moved in I'd ordered a Ballantine whisky against the cold and one for her too on my bill. Then a phone-call informed me of an invitation to the Czech Club, preceded by a tour of the sites of London . . . I was accompanied by the photographer Kaplan with his fiancée, Polka, a Czech actress who still pined for Prague, for she used to play at the Reduta jazz club, but that was quite a while back . . . First we stopped in front of the University, where long long ago Karl Marx started to write *Das Kapital*. On the wall there's an oval plaque with his name and date of birth, and the period of his residence in London. But I wanted to take a tour round all the places where the poet T. S. Eliot lived and went, I'd already been to Oxford University where Eliot studied, where I'd visited not only his College, but also its magnificent dining-hall in the shape of an upturned ship.

Dubenka, now in Oxford, this was on the third day of my visit to England, I caught such a chill, I never recovered from it. I was the guest of the head of the Czech department, they invited me into their common room, there were armchairs, so I warmed myself up a bit in those armchairs, we even had a kind of seminar, washing it down with whisky. Every teacher had keys to a certain cupboard, where there were little sliding racks like in a bar, and there in a row stood bottles of every sort and kind. But the head just picked one bottle without a name and said, this one certain distilleries make just for themselves, apparently he got this special brand of whisky as a favour. And it was quite outstanding, maybe just because it had no name. Then they took me off round that great University town, it was bitterly cold, we were looking for the window out of which a certain student used to recite *The Waste Land* through a megaphone every evening at dusk, but we couldn't find it, so I simply decided what with the cold and that, and I pointed . . . There's our window, and that's that! And so I cut short my Oxford torment. Then we went out for dinner. There were at least thirty of us round the table, so it was even quite warm, because thirty people give out a fair degree of heat, in other words, round the table there sat thirty night-storage heaters with a temperature of thirty six degrees Celsius . . . and the food was hot, Indian, and as by now I had the flu, I warmed myself up with the spicy hot food and liquor . . . And again, Dubenka . . . Being a guest of the University I slept in a special room for distinguished visitors . . . but as I inched myself into the folded back blankets, I discovered that the sheets were as icy as Priessnitz's compress, which Francin my dad used to give me in the Nymburk brewery during my forty-degree fevers. There was nobody about in the building, and I didn't know how to find those stairs to the common room where we'd had our discussion, the one with the sideboard whose sliding shelves held those rows of whisky bottles. So there I lay, too afraid to move, I'd gone to bed fully dressed, but the cold overpowered my pyjamas, my sweaters, and my jacket . . . and I imagined with horror how on the third day I'd get pneumonia, but I survived that too . . . The main thing was, to have been to Oxford, where T. S. Eliot once studied . . .

And later, going round London, I sat in the car with my new friends, who'd warmed to me and my books, and we stopped outside a certain suburban house with an oval plaque on the front wall saying the poet T. S. Eliot had lived here . . . Affected by this, I had my photograph taken, then we returned on foot to the corner of the street — and there was the pub where the poet used to go for a pint with his son . . . After that we sped on through the streets to a certain bank with another oval plaque, saying that the poet T. S. Eliot had worked here for forty years . . . Then we drove across the Thames, to the spot where that theatre once stood where William Shakespeare lived and performed with his company, but quite recently the remains had been obliterated, the bulldozers had laboured away in the face of protests from actors throughout the world . . . Richard Burton himself lay down in front of one bull-dozer, but they soon carted him off . . . So now only the original dressing rooms remain in tiny George Inn Yard, a pub with long first-floor galleries where even now on special anniversary days certain Shakespeare plays are performed.

We entered this multiple-chambered timber inn, it was like five Golden Tigers run together, we ordered our Guinness, and it was almost as cold in there as it was in that bed for honoured guests in Oxford . . . these days coaches come to that tiny remaining historic yard, and foreigners photograph every nook and cranny. My friends told me about some fellow from the North of England who'd come to work in the nearby shipyards, but after a month he'd lost nearly two stone in weight, so he set off to go back north where he came from. They showed me the famous hill above the city, today it's a beautiful park, where he'd met this cat on the road, heading south, in the opposite direction, and the tom cat gave the haggard fellow such a queer look that he decided to go straight back to London with the cat . . . once more to seek his fortune by the banks of the Thames . . . and together they won this fortune, — in less than ten years that cat and he became rich, and he became the most famous Lord Mayor of London . . . Mr Kaplan told me this story tenderly, and we ordered more Guinness, a dark beer with almost centimetre-thick coffee-coloured foam right to the brim . . . Mr Kaplan took a match, and dipping it in the thick foam, he drew a four-leaved clover, saying shamrock was the Irish emblem, and this is what you do in Ireland, you sip it slowly, you

sup it, you don't gulp it down like you do in Prague or Bavaria . . .
so we drank it slowly, and that four-leafed clover, as if embossed
in the foam by the match, slowly dropped down, and when we'd
drunk up, that four-leafed clover lay on the bottom of the glass as
if it was made out of coffee nougat . . . So we had ourselves another
round of Guinness, and for luck I drew a four-leafed clover into
my own foam with a match . . . but Shakespeare's pub was starting
to fill up with foreigners, so we set off again on this quest of mine
for *The Waste Land*, for I'd found a dozen localities in the text I
needed to visit, since Eliot loved London the way Joyce loved
Dublin . . . I suppose London must be just as colourful a city as
your own San Francisco, Dubenka, but the chill of the place
enhances the nip of the colours, wherever you look Impressionist
canvases just leap out at you, the soaring expressivity forces you to
wipe your eyes, the dazzle gives you conjunctivitis, reflexes of
colour and light, closing and opening of windows, like the weld-
ing of steel track . . . and those parks, whole meadows several miles
long, planted with great round flower-beds decorated like cakes,
and to make you taste the whole zest of this city, the avenues are
forever impeded by roundabouts, every few hundred yards you
have to follow all the other cars round in a circle . . . and taxi drivers are particularly held in awe, main road or side road, it's just
eyeball to eyeball! . . . But those gardens and parks . . . Twice that
day we saw the sun come out, and instantly the mile-long parks
were peppered everywhere with people lying about on the green,
just as they were, fully dressed, lying back to present their faces
even for one short hour to the sun, which really blazes forth just
for a time, till your eyes half-close . . . It's part of a general phe-

nomenon, in other ways too, all the kids go about in shorts, while I'm shivering bitterly with cold . . . it's May, and the lovers go to the groves so gay . . . London has dozens and dozens of square miles of such groves . . . it was even pointed out to me that one lovely big park on the way to the Tate Gallery, belongs exclusively to the residents, whose windows look out on to this park and its benches, and every occupant has a key to the lock on the gate . . . to anyone else entry is prohibited . . . A moment later the sky is overcast, the sunbathers leap up to sit on the park benches or walk on their way refreshed . . . And next, as requested, Dubenka, we drove over to King William Street . . . over the bridge, as it appears in *The Waste Land* . . . "Unreal city,/ Under the brown fog of a winter dawn,/ A crowd flowed over London Bridge, so many,/ I had not thought death had undone so many . . ." There I quoted my T. S. Eliot, and a moment later we were listening through the open car window to where, as the poet accurately describes it . . . "Saint Mary Woolnoth kept the hours/ With a dead sound on the final stroke of nine . . ." I was quoting badly, but still, from memory, those lines from The Burial of the Dead . . . the first chapter of *The Waste Land* . . . then we leant over the wall by the Thames, the dull water flowed, emitting its damp whiff . . . and I cited . . . "The nymphs are departed./ Sweet Thames, run softly, till I end my song./ The river bears no empty bottles, sandwich papers,/ Silk handkerchiefs, cardboard boxes, cigarette ends/ Or other testimony of summer nights. The nymphs are departed./ And their friends, the loitering heirs of City directors,/ Departed, have left no addresses./ By the waters of Leman I sat down and wept . . ." I recited these lines to my friends, and we watched the sweet

Thames, as it ran softly, till I ended my song . . . Then we drove on this way and that, finally discovering that Eliot was correctly inspired after all . . . We located that Cannon Street Hotel to which the partner was asked by "Mr. Eugenides, the Smyrna merchant/ Unshaven, with a pocket full of currants . . ." we'd found the Cannon Street Hotel, what more could I ask. And quite soon, Dubenka, as Mr Kaplan the photographer and I have promised, we'll go to Dublin and stroll about there like Joyce . . . like Ulysses . . . for one week we'll take the local cure, on foot, drinking nothing but Guinness in Ormond's Bar . . . Then we looked for and found the embankment in *The Waste Land* by Queen Victoria Street . . . and we found the bar in Lower Thames Street . . . and we peered up at the tower of the church, "where the walls/ of Magnus Martyr hold/ inexplicable splendour of Ionian white and gold . . ." Then I wanted to follow on in the wake of the lines . . . "Highbury bore me. Richmond and Kew/ Undid me. By Richmond I raised my knees/ Supine on the floor of a narrow canoe./ My feet are at Moorgate, and my heart/ Under my feet . . ." but my friends burst out laughing . . . no, that's too far, way out past Kew Gardens, next time you'll have to come for a whole week, Mr Hrabal . . . So I said: Then where are those lines . . . "On Margate Sands./ I can connect/ Nothing with nothing./ The broken fingernails of dirty hands . . ."? No. We've got to go now, Robert's expecting us at the Czech Club, besides, we're hungry . . . And I said: I'm hungry too, not to mention freezing cold, but I must just finish this one off, while my memory still serves me . . . "I sat upon the shore/ Fishing, with the arid plain behind me/ Shall I at least set my lands in order? . . . These fragments I have shored against my ruins . . .

Hieronymo's mad againe . . ." And my friends laughed, and we drove off through the motley streets and gardens, past the parks and hedges and bushes in bloom, and my friends laughed . . . Sure, Hieronymo's mad againe . . . That's our Robert all right, he'll be deep in his cups by now . . .

The Czech Club's in a residential area, there's been a restaurant here ever since the premises were acquired in the days of the First Republic, we didn't reach the place till two, but we still got fed, — pork, dumplings and sauerkraut, two Gypsies were playing away in the club room, on cimbalom and fiddle, there were three people in there, dressed up smart, in their Sunday best, with President Masaryk's portrait hanging on the wall in its golden frame, we had our meal, and Robert came over, bawling vociferously, blazing with vigour, proudly reporting that last week some Irishmen had come over the fence, and Robert had managed to beat them senseless . . . And sure enough Robert was deep in his cups by now, but everyone loved him, writhing with laughter as he yarned on about his youth in Bohemia, and his grandmother and his mother, but I couldn't follow a word, he was so convulsed with delight in his own narrative, all this laughter and roaring was really a kind of therapy, and then we went out into the shabby garden, just tables, poles stuck in the ground with planks on them, and everywhere bottles of Czech Pilsner, 75-centilitre best Export stuff, Robert had his own audience, he weighed a ton and he carried on enthusing, squeaking and roaring, emitting the varied noises of an express train, the sun came out, and still we sat there as Robert performed away, I drank my beer and gave up listening, unable to decipher the semantic load of Robert's antics, while other

Sunday regulars arrived, dapper in all their smart togs, drinking their three-quarter-litre bottles of Pilsner they followed perfectly all of Robert's enthusings shrouded in cat's cradles of laughter . . . in the end I even had to laugh myself . . .

Another thing . . . over the fence there lived numerous families of Mohammedans, ten curly children's heads were gaping there in big-eyed astonishment at all these goings-on in the Czech Club, all that ecstasy and laughter and squealing of mirth and fist-blows to the table delivered by that enthused high-spirited Robert . . . a young lassie turned up with a dog, which proceeded to do its business, and the garden greatly amused itself at the expense of this growing girl, who finally took some newspaper and wrapped the dog turd up and red with shame she carried it off to a rubbish bin, while Robert continued his babble of lingoes derived from the Tower of Babel, the photographer Mr Kaplan said Robert was just a great big child, a real kind-hearted soul, and, as I'd already noticed, a fine dancer, who entranced less by his shouting than by the dance-like gestures with which he accompanied these drunken revels . . . and Robert embraced everyone present, falling off his chair, sitting down and missing his seat, — all week they looked forward to his clowning show, he gave regular performances every Sunday afternoon . . . and I took a look about me . . . once it must've been a proper garden restaurant, the kind we used to have in Prague suburbs, or in the Sudetenland . . . they used to have billiards too . . . but everything was ripped out, gone to rack and ruin, but this decayed quality didn't bother anyone . . . quite the reverse, they all felt as if they were back in Prague in some identical shabby one-time garden restaurant . . . some of the regulars sat inside, togged out in their Sunday afternoon best, with the fiddle and cimbalom playing, there were even a few Hungarians . . . but not Slovaks, they don't come, I was told, they have another smart restaurant, the Irish particularly like it, they really love the place, consuming gallons of Pilsner interspersed with Irish whiskey . . . And President Masaryk in his golden frame grips his left wrist with his right hand, the way Andy Warhol liked to have his photograph taken, — he's a bit fed-up, he wouldn't like this cimbalom and fiddle music all mixed up with Robert's roaring and his grotesque dancing tripody . . . I was starting to go off it too, only the ten little heads leaning with their elbows flat on the garden wall went on gaping in wonder at that scene in the Czech former restaurant garden, where Robert bellowed and guffawed and constantly subsided from his chair . . . The sun went down, — and again a chill ran right through me, it was "May, cold May", and by rights, "in the barn a heaven of hay", but there I was sitting with all these smiling Czechs, the lassie walked about with her huge dog in this former garden, and I felt miserably cold . . . all I wanted was to take the shortest way home, to get back to the hotel, sit in the plush armchair and warm my back and gaze out at the lamp-lit boulevard, at the avenue, watching London's Sunday night-life through those glass doors and wall . . . so my friends took me back, we said goodbye, and I slumped into my seat, while the black girl in her apron with a huge bow brought me a large whisky, and I ordered her a big one as well, and she was pleased I had eyes for her too . . .

Yet our President hadn't been left entirely alone and bereft there in the Czech Club. Many a time in that afternoon I'd sat

back-to-front on my chair and gazed into Masaryk's sad visage, —
and he wasn't alone, two Gypsies played for him on the cimbalom
and the violin, handsome and smart they were with their oiled hair,
and the stand-up fiddler, the *Stehgeiger*, he looked as if he was playing right into the President's ear, playing those Moravian Slovak
songs which Masaryk loved so well, and as for me, when the bow
attained its summit, only to slide right down the strings to the
Gypsy's waist, I shed tears as always . . . "The water it runs and it
runs, past the manor, and further . . . the tears I've wept and I've
shed, I who was once the lover . . ." And out in the garden Robert
really just enhanced and spurred on those two Gypsies, with all his
inhuman shouting and tumbling, as they played religiously away
for those Hungarians, but also for me . . . and for the President
. . . in that Czech Club, where Robert beat nearly ten Irishmen
senseless for climbing over the garden fence . . .

After thawing out at the hotel I went back out on to
Birmingham Street, boarded the first bus that came and rode it out
to the terminus, — what a sight, what an experience! It was late
Sisley and Manet, Pissarro, all those Impressionist paintings of
atmospheric city scenes, where crowds of people slowly but surely
shade into the shapeless throng, this was a constant succession of
colour and sound, I rode out into these constant concatenations,
those Correspondances, as Charles Baudelaire wrote in the poem,
of colours and scents and notes, which all correspond, — and I
realised how and why the metropolis draws people in from the
country, it's a great symphony to ride along upstairs in a double-
decker bus and look out the window in front, and behind, turning
around, and sideways . . . everywhere I'm assailed by this cruel,

inhuman, yet stunning world for the human eye, for the person who wants to be alone, who is alone, even when he's surrounded by all that makes Paris Paris and London London.

As the bus drove past the fountains in Trafalgar Square I was struck by something, something I'd never remembered before . . . When I was young, I did my national service in Olomouc, in the one-time Maria Schnee Kaserne, the barracks where Uncle Pepin had also served under Austria-Hungary, I was in the artillery, with the horses, and once for failing to tighten a saddle strap properly and falling off on exercise in front of an officer I was punished by being sent to man the shovels . . . which meant, Dubenka, that you had to stay overnight in the army stables with this shovel thing, and whenever some horse or mare started to pee, I, doctor-of-law and poet-in-the-making, had to take the shovel and stick it under the horse's privates, or the mare's tail, and wait until those army horses had finished their business . . . except that as soon as one got started, army horses' poetic associations being what they are, off went another . . . and there I was, rushing with my shovel from one horse to another . . . next morning the sarge would yell at me and I'd have to lay out fresh straw for the horses and lug the wet stuff off for compost . . . that's the odd memory which came to me, Dubenka, as I rode through Sunday night-time London . . . And likewise, once when I was sent to Soběslav on the artillery course, again . . . when they gave us our assignments, three times it fell to me to go to the military hospital in Tábor . . . it looked simple enough . . . it was the Ward for Bed-Wetting National Servicemen . . . and I had the fairly straightforward task — of waking up those servicemen in time, before they could wet themselves . . . but

always, just like those military mares and geldings, I would wake a
man up just after he'd wetted himself, or the doctor on military
service would tear a strip off me for failing to wake up the poor
sick bed-wetting servicemen because I was fast asleep myself . . .
Come clean, soldier! . . . And I did . . . And again, Dubenka, during that lovely Impressionist bus journey of mine another place
came to mind . . . the Maria Schnee Kaserne . . . In Rome there's
this particular church, before they started building it, they waited
for the first snows to fall, thinking how lovely that church would
be up on a hill, how very beautiful . . . so there where the first snow
fell and lay, they built this holy place in honour of the Virgin Mary
. . . Mary of the Snows, Maria Schnee . . . and following in the steps
of the one in Rome another one in Olomouc . . . Finally I got out
at the terminus and I boarded another bus to take me the two-hour
journey back, — Well, Dubenka, what fun and games I had in
London . . .

The double-decker bus followed its route back, and the streets
and squares were so full of people out taking their leisure, that even
that bright-coloured day hardly rolled along, it slowed down, people weren't in a hurry to get anywhere . . . my bus circled Nelson's
Column at a walking pace, there are four giant lions at its foot, and
there in the day and in the evening dozens of children are always
sliding about on these lions, these lions were crawling with them,
like the river god of the Nile, the kids rode them as if they were
on slides in the park, again and again, those bodies of couched lions
with their paws before them were even polished, gleaming, and,
Dubenka, I couldn't help remembering our Old Town Square in
Prague, that monument to Jan Hus, which ever since the Velvet

Revolution has been crawling with young people, all over the steps, even on the plinth, anywhere you can sit, you find these young people, Master Jan Hus has rock groups in front of him, young people sitting on the steps writing postcards and greetings from Prague on their knees, even quite tiny children under the eyes of their parents scrambling up under the auspices of various gaunt ascetic mystics, who ushered our nation into a new era in the name of their revered Master, this monument was a kind of promissory note, redeemable only during the Velvet Revolution, when Rafael Kubelík conducted his symphony orchestra in Smetana's *Má Vlast*, whenever I cross the Old Town Square and see again that monument to Master Jan Hus crawling with its motley folk and clothing, I hear those rock groups, I see those young foreigners sitting on the paving where once the place of execution stood, where those Bohemian Lords were executed in 1621, perhaps only so that finally this freedom, and all of this should belong to the young people . . . often I sit there on a bench and I watch how through the teeming flow of history, the submerged streams of centuries, finally the choral of "Ye Who Are God's Warriors" bursts forth, how with their guitars and their brass the groups express almost the same sentiment that was there at the outset of this nation's history, to which all these young people now belong, thronging the square where once the Bohemian Lords were executed . . . only one of the Lords spoke perfect Czech, the others were German nobility, but they died defying the Habsburgs, just as earlier Master Jan . . . and the Hussites, were victorious for so many years, that in the end they defeated themselves somewhere out in the fields by Lipany . . .

Dear Dubenka, when I got back to my hotel in Birmingham

Street and sat down in my warm armchair in the foyer, I found a Czech emigré waiting for me there, the poet Ivan Jelínek, he gave me his two books of verse, I took a look, and sure enough, even in emigration the Czech poet had not forgotten that a Czech poet's verse always communicates that urge for Central Europe to tend toward the mystic vision, toward the need for a close attachment to Eastern philosophy, to Indian philosophy . . . the Veda: *T a twam asi* . . . That thou art . . . all people are not only children of God in spirit, but all things living, in nature and man, correspond . . . An elegant old man, the poet Jelínek told me with a smile and with rueful zeal how once he'd had a cattle farm in America, and he'd never needed a whip, for the cows listened to him, and he to them . . . he led them on a string, on a shoelace, feeling united with them, they were his sisters . . . and when the time came for the cows to be sold for slaughter, he fell ill, it was as if he was sending his own children to the slaughterhouse . . . This year and last however he'd been in India, where cows are not only God's own children, but also no-one is allowed to kill them, so they move around among the people, he said, and the poet Jelínek brightened . . . every cow in India has a man to whom she comes at dusk, who is honoured to be allowed to milk her . . . and when the cow is calving, after a while it comes and shows its little calf, its baby, to the man it is attached to . . . Mr Jelínek smiled, he was a poet now, I held open one of his gifts, I felt happy, for the first time, in the company of this poet, I'd truly warmed up . . .

My dear Dubenka, a few days later I paused once more in London in front of a plaque, at number 20 Maresfield Gardens, where it was written in white letters that Sigmund Freud had stayed here in 1938, after fleeing the Nazis in Vienna, I'd been brought here by a young journalist woman, we'd spent ages looking for this house in her car, making a whole string of Fehlleistungen, un-Freudian slips, till finally the young lady had found it. It was closing day. But the young woman rang persistently, and then once again, till a young Indian came out from his lunch, and she said I was a Freudian who'd come all the way from Prague, so the young Indian took us in . . . Today this house is a museum with reading rooms for Freudians, there are studies on the ground and first floor . . . a door opened, and there was Sigmund's study, exactly as it had been in Vienna, with his fin-de-siècle desk and that famous couch, covered in carpet and set with cushions, — the whole of the professor's study displayed a horror of empty space, all the walls were adorned with oriental and contemporary objects and pictures and *objets d'art* . . . we stood there meditatively and imagined a sleeping woman lying on the couch, Sigmund sitting and asking questions in a sonorous voice, and noting down the essence of the somnambulant woman's talk, so that finally Freud would get the picture and find out why the young sleeping woman was neurasthenic, why she suffered from other ailments too, welling up from her psyche. . . . Then Freud's young Indian disciple led us into a lecture room, which was also a cinema, there were about twenty plush chairs in the hall, and there on the white surface of the screen we saw a film about the life of Mr Sigmund Freud in Vienna . . . Freud didn't like being filmed or having his photograph taken . . . but the loveliest thing in the film was, that of all living things Sigmund liked his two chow-chow dogs the best, otherwise he was very solemn in the film, but when he was with his little dogs he laughed, several times showing the camera not only those little chow-chows, but himself with them . . . at home, in the garden, on the balcony, he lifted them up together and shook them in front of the camera, laughing and beaming with delight, that was his joy, that those little Chinese mutts, once bred at home for slaughter, for their excellent meat, had been trained by himself, humanised, by psychoanalysis, no doubt, till they laughed with him into the camera . . . That moved me to tears . . . And then the young Indian told us about how, during the last year of his life, Freud only left his villa to try to find someone to take care of his pet chow-chow . . . the surviving one he'd brought to London . . . and a year later he died . . . We returned through Freud's living quarters and bedroom, there were photographs in the connecting passage, one of which truly gripped me, an X-ray photograph of Freud's skull, side on, where you saw how for seventeen years the cancer had eaten away his cheek bones with its automatic writing . . . and again! Salvador Dali. All his life he'd longed to meet Freud, he'd visited him several times in Vienna, but he'd never succeeded in meeting his beloved Freud, till here in London, where he did this drawing, in which the portrait of a scientist emerges from its lines of force, a drawing created by the paranoiac-critical method, containing the whole fate of the man, whom the Surrealists considered so much their spiritual father that they took this scientist, whose method in *The Interpretation of Dreams*, and *Studies on Hysteria*, was close not only to André Breton or Salvador Dali, but all the Surrealists, and when assembling a group picture of all the Surrealists, as well as putting in Dostoyevsky they added Sigmund Freud . . . who, as you know, Dubenka, was born in Moravia . . . and the young Indian told me, interpreted by the journalist, that next year was the 135th anniversary of Freud's birth, a conference was to be held in Prague, he'd invite me to it . . . And he took down my address, while I sweated to think how I'd lied, saying I was a Czechoslovak pupil of Freud, but the Indian hadn't guessed a thing . . .

Dear Dubenka, another ideal spot for a honeymoon is Bristol. Here I was so incredibly cold, that during the afternoon I totally lost track of my genitals. The wintry air clarified the outlines of this former spa, the shadows of the houses were so dark, that the sunlit walls dazzled, and as the rhododendrons were in bloom, and it was a city of villas and little villa-like houses and the sea was close by, the air was bracing as beef soup. Here I had a talk at the University, but this University consists of nothing but villas, large villas, a bit like the ones our magazine *Young World* publicised recently in an almost ten-page spread, — the villas of former politicians and other erstwhile influential persons, who obtained by improper means just such villas as those in Bristol which house the Russian Department, which naturally includes Czech studies. When I entered one classroom in this Department, I was surprised by how unsurprised the two young teachers of Czech with me were — the whole decoration was Soviet, the place was all adorned with posters and busts, just like those Soviet films on the life of Komsomol youth. We chatted, I was freezing cold, and we waited for the Head of Department to arrive. He was a Russian, with all that goes with it, the kind of well-fed Russian we come across in Prague. It was he who introduced me to the dozen or so students of Czech, it was he who posed me the questions . . . and I replied in the manner of my *Dodgings on a Pocket Handkerchief* . . . in other

words, if asked: Have you ever swum in the river Maltsch? I'd reply
. . . Never, but the Turkish Sultan was a great guy . . . And having
with me, Dubenka, a case full of my *November Hurricanes*, I replied
exclusively, as if deaf, on what I'd seen and experienced during the
November Hurricane . . . In less than an hour I was so freezing
cold, that I thanked them prematurely, saying: Depart, dear com-
rades, unto thy shacks. I conclude. Yours truly! Then I shook the
Russian's hand and praised him for leaving his Russian
Department's wall decorations so prudently the way things used
to be, in the days of poster-caparisoned walls . . .

And we drove off through the town, the streets were like long
concertina books on the subject of working-class dwellings, and
white-collar villas, and prosperous main roads sloping down to the
port. I was fascinated again by the liking for flowers and fine meadows in the middle of town, parks in which even today according to
municipal laws anyone could graze his goats or sheep free of charge
. . . Again we passed through beautiful avenues, festooned with
flower beds and bushes of blooming laburnum and rhododendron.
We stopped by a great bridge, paid our toll and crossed that gigantic bridge, a bit like the one in Bratislava. Down below was a black
river bed, pitched with mud, hill sides full of fresh bushes and trees,
my friends told me there were caves beneath the cliff where even
today a hermit lives, also it's a favourite bridge for suicides . . . I
said, Russian-wise: *A vody nyet*! . . . No water! . . . and my friends
said that was the whole charm of Bristol, once it had been a spa
town, a watering-place like Carlsbad, but the doctors had decided
the mineral waters were bad for your health, whisky and beer were
better . . . so the spa had turned into a place for tennis . . . I

repeated: But, *vody nyet*! . . . Not now, it's low tide, they explained. Bristol is famous for its hundreds of little boats waiting at the mouth of the river for the tide to come in, and then the boaters get in their boats, and the current carries them fifteen miles and more upstream, inland, where there are restaurants and bistros, and there the trippers get out and lark about till the tide begins to turn. Then they jump in their boats, and the tide takes them back down again, past the lovely banks to the mouth of the river . . . Young people like to come here on their honeymoons, Dubenka, so we too, when our time comes, shall ride up with the tide in a garlanded boat with our friends to the restaurant where the wedding feast awaits us . . .

And the breeze blowing up with a stench of mud was so great and icy, that the cold made me want to jump, right down into the mud . . . and the wife of my guide and host from the Czech section said: It's getting a bit chilly. Let's go and warm up at the Bear . . . So we went back to where the bridge ends and those beautiful avenues begin, parked the car, and went into the Bear to warm up, into this old pub, the oldest in Bristol . . . And like practically every other pub, it was even colder inside than it was outside . . . Two customers were sitting beneath the window at an oak table on oak chairs, the barman carefully wiped the glasses and raised them to the light, like the priest raising the chalice at mass, then once again with a napkin he carefully wiped each glittering glass . . . And my friends smiled in response to my dazed face . . . All over the walls and ceiling, all over the place there were stuck up and pinned with tacks cases and boxes of buttons of all sizes, for several maybe decades on end the landlord had amused himself with this collage of buttons of all kinds and all makes, not merely English, but Continental firms too . . . I even saw above me the name of our very own firm from back home, Koh-i-Noor Waldes . . . it was a kind of cavern, in which instead of water there on the gleaming walls you saw row upon row of cards and cases of pearly and metal buttons of all sizes, buttons for all kinds of uniforms, all kinds of children's, men's and ladies' clothing and dresses, for bed linen and quilt covers . . . and the varied colours of all those adornments and uniform requirements . . . There was a passage into a parlour, maybe a club room, where girl students were sitting, with their knees drawn in, to ward off the cold, then you went straight into a garden, where there were tables and chairs, and the sun was still shining . . . and here we sat, it was less chilling out here than it was in that main room, which looked like something set up in homage to our own Jiří Kolář, in its resemblance to all his assemblages and collages . . . Then we got warm in the only way possible, downing more and more beer, and dining on what we'd omitted to have in Scotland . . . boiled mutton with hot potatoes, drowned in mint sauce . . .

Afterwards we drove to a theatre, where all available surfaces were draped with scenery under construction, made out of pressed wires and bars, maybe it was supposed to evoke a prison scene, the woman making the set was swathed in a double layer of tracksuit, and as she carried the pots of paint about and painted the recumbent scenery with her brush, I thought she was smoking, but it was only steam coming from her mouth . . . And my hosts had me look at a poster displayed in the foyer — three years ago in honour of Václav Havel, who'd been in jail at the time, they'd performed his play here . . . *Largo Desolato* . . .

Finally we stopped in another pub, where smugglers met, it was like another three whole Golden Tigers stuck together, decorated with rare candlesticks and pans and so on . . . but there was nobody in it . . . we went through the kitchen, but there was nobody there either . . . so off we went to the railway station . . . And Dubenka! There in the train it was warm at last! I was saved . . . A pity we didn't burn to death instead! Mind you my frozen genitals didn't thaw out till we got to London . . .

Kersko, 8th-9th September 1990

Total Fears

And a young woman came to the Tiger and introduced herself, saying she was a Danish journalist and writer, and she'd like to do an interview with me . . . her other half was standing behind her, both were indeterminate in age . . . and I was sitting with Motýlek — Papillon — and his pal Pepík Jáchym, who'd received so many stab wounds all over his body, that he could say of himself what Andy Warhol said, after being shot by Valerie Solanes, that his body was so peppered with shots, it looked like a beautiful dress from Dior . . . up till his wounding Pepík Jáchym had worked as a bodyguard, and he'd been off sick for over two months, but now he was mending . . . so there we sat, being annoyed by this painter fellow Macků, who kept butting in with his dreadful incoherent chat . . . and sitting with me, Dubenka, was Mr Smoljak from the theatre, whom I introduced when we arrived as . . . Svěrák & Smoljak . . . and Mr Smoljak objected . . . I'm only Smoljak, my dad's a Sub-Carpathian Ruthenian, like Andy Warhol's dad . . . and so this journalist woman came and we pushed aside our turbulent painter Macků, objecting he was though, blabbering away, a total idiot, till Motýlek indicated he would intervene . . . backed up by Pepík Jáchym, that strongman, massive chest, in his shirt sleeves, half recovered by now . . . so I shoved aside Mr Macků, raving away in his splendid drunken stupor, I sat that journalist down beside me, and she put me her questions . . . but Macků kept sticking his oar in, leaning over and breathing fetid beer fumes in her face . . . till my bodyguard pal got to his feet, lightly lifted up that great drunken painter Mr Macků, held him by the scruff of his coat and trousers, and carried him like a child through the bar and out in front of the pub . . . he plonked him down, came back and seated himself once more . . . and Motýlek was glad he wasn't the one who'd had to dispose of Mr Macků . . . and Mr Smoljak ate his plate of scrag end and wondered at this stuff I had to put up with, we'd just come in from Kersko where he'd ambushed me with a film crew, and I'd shouted at them, saying I'd just had pneumonia, but then I relented, and to avoid them tramping over my living-room, I stuck a rug on the bench and shouted to that crew of film people, actually it was only a young lady and one fellow with a camera and another with a microphone . . . and Mr Smoljak himself, who asked me questions on the subject of 'What Is Czech Humour' . . . and that's just the subject for me, I know it off by heart . . . a couple of telegraphic mentions of Kafka, and Hašek, and Prague irony . . . and then we drove into Prague by van, there was this draught down my back and I'd forgotten my scarf . . . so I could feel my back chilling, the blasted driver had his little side-window open, and I was right behind him . . . So Mr Smoljak understood why I'd spoken so rudely in the mini-van, and especially here in the Tiger, when, for the second time running, our black-haired giant Jáchym, like some great Soviet weight-lifter . . . had to take that heavy painter Macků, totally sozzled, haul him out bodily through the bar again, and toss him gently on to the pavement . . . and nobody was surprised, nobody was put out, my friend Motýlek — Papillon — he didn't excite himself either, he who'd done nine years for accidentally killing a policeman and used to have a butterfly tattooed on both earlobes, like Steve McQueen . . . but he's had one removed now he wants to be normal again, this tenderly aggressive person . . .

And the Danish journalist, who looked like a woman from Dullsville joining a queue for meat or something equally precious, she sat there asking me questions, and I was showing off in front of Mr Smoljak, whose dad, like Andy Warhol's father, was a Sub-Carpathian Rusín, Ruthenen in German, I was showing off to him, and those two giants of mine, my bodyguards, they smoked and listened, gazing over to the bar from the great antlers, and I replied in German to the Danish lady, who eventually got to her final summing-up question . . . So, you say, while other writers suffered in jail as dissidents and members of Charter 77, you were having a good time . . .? I said . . . Oh, you mean, did I groan and suffer and was I interrogated, but, my dear Danish lady, that was a matter of course . . . the way I used to be summoned and slowly but systematically gently tormented by the officers of our humane police . . . that was just part of one's civic rights and duties, there's nothing about it in the constitution of course, but whichever of my friends was and is sensitive, touchy even, had to choose . . . emigration . . . and I emigrated inwardly, here to the pub for example . . . And, my dear Danish lady, how awfully afraid I used to be, and how even today I am horribly afraid! My mother was so terribly afraid all her life, she used to be so afraid . . . but today she isn't, because she's dead . . . the dead have peace . . . You see — my mother told this story of herself — one Sunday, when I was still in my mother's womb, my impetuous grandpa dragged my mother out into the yard just before lunch, with me still inside her, he pulled out a gun and roared . . . Kneel, I'm going to shoot! And my mother, a grown-up little girl, clasped her hands and begged for me . . . Finally my grandmother came out and said . . . Come in and eat, or it'll all get cold! So in we went to eat, my Danish lady, and here I am . . . but that fear stayed with me, felt through the womb of my mother . . . when the boys on Balbínova called me over and knocked me into a porch and threatened me with a pistol, a pop-gun, I went crazy with horror, with a fearful horror, subconsciously I saw my granddad's gun aimed against me . . . and the boys squeezed the trigger . . . and I experienced my own death, even though it was only a cork flying at me on the end of a piece of string . . . So, my Danish lady, now you see how afraid I can be . . . and yet I didn't emigrate, though I was so afraid . . . just as everybody is in fact . . .

And you ask, how did I overcome so easily the totalitarianism of the last twenty years? Right now . . . This will actually be a confession about my fear . . .

One time for example my wife and I were meant to be travelling with some friends to Greece . . . Husák was in control by then, nineteen seventy-something . . . I'd applied for the exit permit, I kept going there and asking, to no avail, by now it was the day before our flight, and still there was nothing . . . So I went to the passport and visa office, somewhere about Bartolomějská, and there I witnessed a wonderful scene, one young man, who was also supposed to be flying the next day, and still had nothing, he dragged an official out of his office by the jacket and shook him and roared at him and shook his fist, saying if he didn't get it by this afternoon he'd kill him, with this very fist he was brandishing in front of his face, he'd kill him . . . and we were shaking, he'd done this instead of us . . . and when our turn came two hours later the official said I wouldn't be getting it till the next day, the chief wanted to speak to me personally . . . And I was dying with fear, my wife was tearing a strip off me for being fit only for beer drinking and nothing else . . . I arrived with my nerves going to pieces, dreading what would happen, and I waited in that office, and a car came, a police Volga, and I was driven through Prague by men who couldn't have been anything other than secret police . . . they took me over to that tile-clad Interior Ministry block by Letná, just so Pipsi and I could get our passport and exit permit . . . up the lift in that tile-clad edifice, a system of doors, led all the while by these young men, like a dance committee, all smiles and politeness, and slapping on the back, then a door flew open, light, a view out the window over to the Sparta stadium and the Castle, and there sat a fat man in a smart off-the-peg suit, smiling at me, I sat down opposite him, my nerves were going to pieces with trepidation . . . and he stroked the back of my hand and straightened his tie, his hair was oiled . . . and I saw those who had brought me sitting in a corner, with a view of the Castle, sitting and flicking matches, playing matchboxes, flipping a box of matches up in the air, thrilled or disappointed according to which way it fell . . . and that smiling official stroked the back of my hand, and I, though it was summer and I was sunburnt, felt myself pale . . . Suddenly he banged his fist on the table and bellowed . . . So what do you want?! Do you want to be friends with that writer Vaculík, or do you want to go to the beach in Salonika?! . . . And he looked at me and I went paler still and stammered . . . My wife . . . He banged on the folder and exclaimed . . . We know all about her, her stuff's here as well . . . And he struck his hand again on the big folder . . . I said: But we only want to go on holiday to the sea, to Salonika . . . And again that official roared, while his subordinates carried on, passionately involved with their matchboxes, I stammered: But I'm not particularly friends with Vaculík . . . I have other friends . . . And the official banged his hand again on another folder . . . That's all here too, subversive stuff, dissident tendencies, so what do you want!? . . . Vaculík, or Salonika? . . . Salonika, I said . . . He laughed and handed me my passport, with the tip of an exit permit poking out . . . And then he said, with infinite bonhomie . . . Just as I thought . . . I mean, you're a writer, know what I mean, but who is that Vaculík fellow? Sure, he gets money from abroad . . . but what's he compared with someone like you . . . you are and will be a writer . . . I'm a doctor of philosophy, I promise you, you'll be published again, you'll be a proper author, not like him . . . the crook! . . . he exclaimed, shaking his fist, doubtless in the direction of Vaculík's abode . . . But I had my passport and exit permit, the Interior officials were still engrossed in their matchbox game, the sun was setting in the west . . . and that official, that doctor of philosophy, he slapped me friendly-like on the back, horror flowed over me, I can't stand that sort of thing, I'm like Cézanne in that respect, whenever anyone so much as touched him, he never spoke to them again . . . but I wanted an exit permit for myself and my wife, so I put up with it, that false friendly slap on the back . . . then he leant over me, he put his lips to my ear, and he whispered . . . You know, you mustn't take it like that . . . sometimes we have to shout at you

people . . . but we'll make you a writer yet . . . Boys, take the maestro home . . .! He instructed, and the boys stopped their matchbox
game, actually they weren't playing, only pretending . . . the two
of them looked like assistants from Kafka's *The Castle*, the assistants of K. the land-surveyor.

So I got to go to the seaside, to Salonika, and Mount Athos as
well . . . My dear Danish lady, that's the start of my little Calvary,
what you call totalism, totalitarianism . . . and now go home, thank
you for making me go back over all those fears and dreads, those
little totalitarities, which might just about have driven me out of
my wits, had it not been for this Velvet Revolution, in which the
actors and the comedians, the students and Mr Gorbachev, over-
threw that mighty power, whose centre was there in the tile-clad
edifice where that slow but monstrous road began which led me
to start contemplating, that rather than be, it would be better not
to be . . .

Back over to our table beneath the great antlers stumbled
painter Macků again, turbulent and sweepingly bewhiskered, claiming a citizen's right to drink his beer, barging his way over to the
table . . . but my protector, my Marlon Brando figure, he merely
smiled, got up, and nobbled the painter, removing first from his
pocket the packet of Sparta cigarettes which Macků had mistak-
enly lifted from the table before his second ousting, then deftly he
carried the painter, arms and legs flailing, out through the Golden
Tiger, and deftly he dumped him outside on the pavement . . . and
Mr Smoljak stroked my hand and stood up, with the Danish writer
and her husband, and he said to me . . . Now I understand, I know
what you mean, Mr Hrabal . . . and he went out of the Golden

Tiger into the dusky twilight . . .

And there in this loud solitude of the Golden Tiger I sizzled with mystery, with *aletheia*, truth, what awaited my head, what I now had to tell, the things I'd actually experienced in that totality, totalitarianism — but I had never known that what I had experienced, this was also totalitarian, I'd actually had it in me all the way from prenatal childhood, from that time in the porch when at the age of six the Balbínova boys shot me with a pop-gun, and I wailed and screamed in the feeling of that horror, which didn't really exist, just like I experienced that horror with the Ministry of the Interior as though it existed, but it didn't, it was only faked . . . and yet, I lived it as if it did exist . . . And now I just exchanged glances with Motýlek and his mate, who once again will work as a night-club bouncer, ah, if you'd seen him the first time he came into the Tiger with his two arms in bandages and wire and splint constructions . . . but, this hero of Tobruk, he drank his beer and smoked, and he dreamed of the time he'd get his destroyed hands on the ones that stabbed him . . . and I told them about how in Kersko, in Mans, in Velenka and especially Manderšejd, there were these regular brawlers, young men who love fighting, not just amongst themselves, but with the police as well, half of these youths are always just out of jail, the other half inside . . . more than anything else they love a good fight with the cops . . . it gets into them all of a sudden, they kick at a police car, rip off the aerial, and haul some policeman out of his vehicle and beat him up, 'coz it's in their blood, it's in their genes . . . one day Mr Novák was unpacking his meat, laying it out on the table in the Hájenka — they'd delivered a week's supply, so he couldn't attend to his customers, but those lads, the brawlers from Mans, and Manderšejd, they came in, wanting to have their beer right away, as they'd just been released from jail . . . but the landlord made a fuss, so these six lads from Mans, from Manderšejd — founded by Prince Alois von Lichtenstein, and called Manderšejd in honour of his wife Karolina, née Sternberg-Manderscheid, a Westphalian family originally, with another Manderscheid in the Rhineland — they got all aggressive, it's just like when Jíra says their village boys never got any further than Jablonec, but on their way there they had to pass Florida, San Francisco, Buffalo Bill and The Cody Inn, fighting the natives all the way — similarly with that Manderscheid background you're compelled to action . . . so the lads from Mans reckoned they'd give old Novák a good belt across the snout, for insulting them, not giving them their drinks right away . . . so they went for him, good and proper, like they did for the cops . . . but Mr Novák called into the corner . . . Mr Daněk, they're trying to beat me up and do me in . . . and there sat Ludva Daněk, meek and mild world discus champion, who offered the fighters of Mans a piece of good advice . . . look here lads, knock it off . . .! And the Manderšejd lads put their heads together and they said . . . What're you farting on about! And Ludva Daněk got to his feet, he was a hundred and thirty kilos, a world champion . . . But that wasn't enough for the Mans boys, they counted themselves and they said . . . Hey, squirt, want a bit of dusting-up, do ya? By this time they were just about to knock Novák to the floor, a hand was hovering over him with a raised log of oak, when two figures got up in a dark corner, they'd been training in Nymburk, like Daněk, and a warning was issued . . . Right now lads, over and above Ludva here you've got the

Svojanovský brothers to deal with . . . The log flew into a corner, hands were raised, and they said . . . Okay okay, we give in, nice to meet you, Mr Daněk, Messrs Svojanovský . . . So we chatted on beneath the great antlers at the Golden Tiger, telling of muscular deeds at the Hájenka inn, but I was still sizzling over everything that had happened to me without my being conscious of it . . . and then other customers came in, but I only nodded, I was somewhere else, back in time, in the depths of time, and I saw all these telegraphic scenes I had witnessed, which I had seemingly forgotten, but they were here with me now, beneath the great antlers in the Golden Tiger . . .

That was the time, when Daněk and the Svojanovský brothers gave me that fine story of strong men in the Hájenka inn, but I used to peregrinate all over the countryside, just entranced by those little winter inns, and those sunken images, which still awake delight in me to this day. We arrive at a pub, inside it's cold, but the innkeeper tosses a tablecloth over us, so we pick any clothes pegs we fancy from the basket and peg ourselves in, so as not to lose that animal warmth, or the warmth we brought from home, then we sit down at the table, there amidst the five ashtrays there's a nappy or diaper pan, and in that pan on the nappies or diapers lies a baby. It smiles, just like that child the monks in Lhasa have in the temple, knowing the child is the measure of all things, and we are just such a child, sitting there in our tablecloths, fastened about with clothes pegs, and the child is heavenly, for the smokers all put their fag ends in the ashtrays, and their matches, and now and then they light some crumpled newspaper, to keep the child from catching a chill . . . and the men grin away, drinking their beer and spirits, and whenever their hands grow numb, they hold their outspread fingers around that nappy or diaper pan . . . Those were the days when Tomorrow would be ours the day after tomorrow, and we would have Everything, *Vsyo boodyet*, and the newspaper *Rudé Právo* was full of prophecies about how Capitalism was bound to be, not simply caught up with, but overtaken . . . so taking those rolled-up newspaper columns we warmed up that diaper pan, mainly to keep the child from getting cold and to have somewhere to warm our hands . . . plenty of beer and spirits were drunk, and the laughs we had! But we had good times in the summer too at the Hájenka. There was one lady who really knew how to pump the beer, as well as look after her mother, Tonička, who only drank green peppermint spirits, and that landlady served a fine goulash, and *utopence*, pickled sausages, but she had a little daughter as well, and in case of need she would bath her wee girl in the sink for the dishes before she washed the plates and cups . . . in the summer she'd give her little girl a bath in the sink where later she rinsed out the glasses . . . that was my golden time, Mr Novák brought order and tidiness to the Hájenka and he could cook great food, while Mr Daněk was still visiting in his red Cortina . . . but then Mr Novák took to the cards a bit, and then he got a bit of a habit of driving off in his car whenever we turned up on our bikes . . . where did he go, that former electricals man, who could make such excellent dishes, bull's testicles and French-style venison lights, from freshly shot roe-deer and wild mouflon . . .?! But! Here I am beneath the great stag's antlers in the Golden Tiger, starting to dream about my totalitarian sufferings, as requested by that Danish lady, in clothes which might have been bought in

Dullsville in the First Republic . . .

And I dreamt vividly of how one of us had a birthday, we'd booked a room at U Sojků, when we started to gather another lot was just leaving after another celebration, and two young men stayed on in the vestibule, totting up the total for the party that was just over . . . Here we gathered, the Society of Friends of Vladimír Boudník, the consultant Franta Mach, my brother and sister-in-law as well . . . and those two in the lobby went on with their adding and multiplying . . . and Mr Hampl hissed . . . Cut my throat and hope to die, those must be secret police . . . and we drank our beer and ate, while those two young men must have had everything counted up ten times over by now . . . and we did our photographs, and Mr Hampl said . . . Cut my throat and hope to die, those two were secret police . . .

And so they were, secret police, next day the phone rang, saying we had to meet, it was in my own interest, otherwise I'd have to be summoned . . . and so we arranged for a meeting the next day in the Belvedere Café, at half past nine . . . And that was a mistake, I should've gone rightaway, I was pale all day, and up all night, imagining the most horrible anti-state activities, subversive, irredentist activities . . . At half past nine I stood there at the counter of the Belvedere Café and recognised him, as we'd agreed, his briefcase was under his arm, and he was blond, even his brows and eyelashes were silvery fair . . . then we sat alone by the window, looking across to Belcrediho . . . and the secret policeman began gently, about how he liked me, how he'd bring me books to autograph, not only for himself, but also for his friends at the office . . . and I was shaking, justifiably as it turned out, for this young man, this official, he told me there'd been a meeting in Prague of some Jazz Section, but it'd been prohibited, and as a gesture of protest we'd met at U Sojků, and I'd been elected its chairman . . . and the official talked knowledgeably and solemnly, but still giving me hope that I was innocent of all this, it was all the fault of Vaculík and Mr Srp, who was publishing these Jazz Section books illegally, and was about to publish my book *I Served the King of England* as well . . . he said he'd like to read it himself and so would his friends at the Ministry . . . And I was horrified, I could see that the waiter was looking at me in the corner, the young man in French piqué could tell how afraid I was, and he knew the man was a secret policeman . . . and when I'd promised that if ever I needed something, an exit permit, say, I'd call the number he gave me, and after thinking it over, I'd ring that number within the next three weeks, and we'd meet up again in front of the Belvedere and go for a walk in the Letná Gardens instead, we descended the steps from the empty Belvedere restaurant, it was ten o'clock, he gave me his clammy hand, like handing me a cold fish . . . and I tottered off in the direction of Strossmayerovo náměstí, while he walked away with his briefcase held tight to his chest, clasped in both hands, and then, just outside the closed wine bar U Poštů, he turned around, aware that I was watching to see where he went . . . I felt years older, my zest for life forsook me, I was miserable and horrified at what I'd got myself into, why had I let myself be drawn into this game, for which I had no desire, which horrified me . . . and now I was trapped . . .

And so we sat together, once a week, the Society of Friends of Vladimír Boudník, in the Plzeňský dvůr, Joska Skalník used to come too, an artist in a black beard and black clothes, he drank red wine and smiled . . . and I told him quietly what it was that was making me pale . . . and Joska waved a hand . . . think nothing of it, our Jazz Section's fully authorised, the European committee has given us their recommendation, in short we've got all the necessary papers . . . We're publishing that *King* of yours . . . And guess where they're printing it? He whispered: We had a couple of drinks with the screws in Pankrác, and they're printing it there, we've shaken hands on the deal, it's just great, isn't it, Mr Hrabal! Nobody can get us for it, we've got all the necessary papers . . . And I was just dying on the spot, and on top it all I added the knowledge that my *King* was now to be printed in Pankrác jail . . .

And that official who gave me the exit permit and passport to Salonika, he used to come and see me every month in Kersko, he was delighted, and being a student of philosophy, he liked to talk to me about my Kant and Schopenhauer, he'd ask after my wife's health, and tell me I had a real future ahead of me, only I had the ability to write a novel stemming from the true life of our people . . . he'd guarantee to give me the kind of advice that would be to my advantage, Vaculík was a rogue, emigrés were sending him money from abroad, Vaculík was a wealthy writer . . . and I sat and looked out the window, and that vain Interior Ministry official was so pleased with himself, he advised me to do plenty of reading, not only of Soviet literature, but also progressive literature from the West . . . his hair was always oiled, he was dapper, and now and then he'd slap me on the back, and half an hour later he'd drive off in his blue Škoda, he used to claim he was visiting his mother somewhere out past Kopidlno, she had a garden and that was his joy and delight, to grow vegetables and restore his energies with practical work, for these were serious times and the burdens of the Interior Ministry were considerable . . . Then, after seeing him off to the gate, I would sit there, unable to do anything, or recall any pleasant memories, I was off the rails . . . and my wife knew it, they visited her as well, now and again, but she always told them to go to hell . . . also the first time she went to see her relatives in West Germany, they advised her to watch out, but not to worry, for the Interior Ministry was vigilant and taking care of her, even in West Germany . . . and one day they told her she could go once every six months, they knew her brother-in-law was a graduate engineer working for a firm in Mannheim, and she could find out certain details . . . But my wife raised her hands and said, in that case she wasn't going anywhere, she wasn't going to be an informer, it wasn't in her character . . . My wife Pipsi . . . She used to advise me, just tell them to piss off! But I had already yielded, I was stuck with it, moreover I was pinned down by Jarda Kladiva, who'd convinced me in the Tiger that he was the one to write my true biography . . . so I brought him all my texts and notes, and we sat together over a beer, sometimes at his place, and through Jarda I got myself back into samizdat, a lady came from some ministry and I gave her the texts and she returned them to me, the original and three copies, and I gave her hundreds of hard-currency vouchers . . . we also had a woman who did the book-binding for us, so now my conscience was further burdened, with that lady who copied forbidden material on fine paper, and that book-binding woman who turned our typescripts into books with fine covers . . . so I spoke politely to the secret police, acted evasive and couldn't wait for the end of every meeting, when I'd be left alone all worried about when we were going to meet again, because I always went and said something or other, so the Interior Ministry officials had me for lunch, sometimes two of them came to the Belvedere, sometimes three, and I autographed my books for them, in cordial friendship, but they went on with indirect questions about where my samizdats were printed, and who supplied the paper, and who I had contacts with . . . and so, for the sake of peace and quiet, I always told them something or other which I regretted later in a state of collapse . . . And I was lucky, too, you see, we used to sit in the Hook, the Krušovická pivnice, where the brew was served by a dead-beat waiter in spectacles, who said he'd dropped out of the Arts Faculty in Bratislava . . . we liked to talk together about philosophy too, especially when he had some time-off in lieu . . . and so the secret police saw me with him, and one day in the Belvedere they got me into a tight corner, said they knew I was keeping it from them, my contact was that waiter in the Hook, with whom I used to discuss philosophy, he was picking up and delivering me those samizdats printed on fine paper . . . I was to tell them the following week how it really was . . . But something totally unexpected happened, that friend of mine, the waiter, he died of diabetes, he was found dead in his room, he was all alone . . . so once again I turned aside from that fate that was lurking in wait for me, the fate of one who betrays and informs on his pals, on people with whom he sits in pubs, and so on . . . But I was shocked by the death of this innocent, and the secret policemen knew it, they even looked forward to my fear and trembling, the bosses actually thought up little ploys to enhance my trepidation . . .

And I couldn't get to sleep without medication, at least with a dose of Rohypnol I got four hours solid sleep, or rather I slipped into unconsciousness . . . I liked to go to bed early, at nine or ten, while my wife stayed up watching TV, after giving me a row for coming home sozzled with beer . . . So one night, when all was quiet in Sokolníky, the bell rings, I totter out and stagger to the door . . . Who is it? I say. And what was it . . . but the police. I opened the door and there was a young policeman, he showed me something he took out of his pocket and informed me that his chief had sent him, he needed to talk to me urgently in the morning . . . there I was in my pyjamas and tousled hair, and the young police-man said in surprise . . . I imagined you quite differently, you're kind of older somehow . . . and look, I was trying to find you in Kersko, I've been everywhere, don't you ever lock the shed? And you just leave your bicycle outside? I stammered, I tottered, and then I asked . . . And how did you get up here, the building's locked . . . He shrugged his shoulders and said . . . That's our prerogative, our secret, here I am and now I'm off . . . So I fell back into bed, my sleep was completely up the spout, I started running through the possible ins and outs of why I had to go and see the chief that morning on Rosenbergových on such important business . . . And in the morning my wife and I took the car, I rang the bell at their headquarters, recalling in shock how once, back in the days when I was a scene-shifter, I popped out to get some beer and just as I was passing their headquarters, it was half past ten, there came a crash of breaking glass, a shadow, and there lying in front of me on the pavement was a young man who'd just jumped out of a fourth-floor window. I stepped back and saw the window was smashed. Then I went and fetched the beer, even in the theatre we could hear the chief yelling at his subordinates . . . then we learnt that during the interrogation someone had fetched the young man a blow and he'd run forward, crouched, and rammed his shoulder through the window, and killed himself . . . and now I was stepping into this building! The policeman on duty telephoned first, then he showed me in and the chief sat me down, looked at me long and hard, and said . . . Who painted your flat . . .? I said, I'll have to think, so I thought, and yes, that was it, it was the time the upstairs neighbour flooded the place, my wife heard in the local pub of someone who did decorating, so she got in touch, and he came and painted the bathroom, and the wife gave him a hundred crowns . . . I said, look, my wife's downstairs, she could tell you all about it . . . So I brought Pipsi up, she told them calmly about the hundred crowns, and the chief told her that the young man was a parasite, who earned a living painting flats and didn't pay any maintenance for his children . . . so they had my wife make a statement . . . and I couldn't drive the car, my wife had to drive, and I was shorter by ten centimetres, in a state of collapse . . . because I like to be afraid, it makes me write better, also writing is my only salvation from that gentle police terror, the lads have got it all worked out . . .

That time, and in the years that followed, whenever I celebrated my birthday, apart from Kosík and Bartošek and Kostroun, and other Dubček advisers and secretaries, Smrkovský the former parliamentary leader was invited out to Kersko as well, to the Hájenka inn, and the police drove out from Prague in two vehicles, and in the middle of the party police officers checked the identities of all those present, including former peasant landholders as well as police assistants from Semice and Velenka, and after all had gone their ways, as described in my memoir volume *Vacant Lots* . . . from time to time an official Volga limousine would come, and when I rode my bicycle, they would drive after me and honk their horn, and I was only going to the Hájenka, or to get some mineral water, so although I only jingled my bicycle bell, I practically flew off into the ditch with the bike, I was shaking so much . . . Sometimes the woman next-door gave me a message . . . Your pals were here again . . . and I knew whose Volga had driven down the tree-lined street, and I felt as if I'd been here, riding my bicycle with them driving along after me . . . Maybe those lads from the Interior Ministry were having fun, even on duty you can always have a bit of fun — at the expense of someone so afraid and scared as me . . . So I was scared not only in Prague, but also in Kersko . . . but of course I went on writing those samizdats of mine . . . One afternoon in the Belvedere the hard boys, my blond chappy, recommended me, they knew I'd do it, to write a letter not only to Vaculík, but also to Havel's brother, saying I didn't want them to distribute my texts in their samizdats . . . and I wrote it, I cobbled together those two letters, I brought them back to the Belvedere, being afraid, and then the blond chap and I took them to the post-office at the end of Belcredka, the blond chap watched as I filled out the address on the registration slip, the one they gave me . . . and then they posted my registered letters themselves in the box . . . and I trotted straight off to U Sojků, where I drank, only to be told off again by my wife in the evening over the TV, for coming home drunk yet again . . . how else! She said to me: But why are you so afraid of them? and I wept at myself for the first time ever . . .

I positively attracted the attentions of the secret police or their assistants. Once I'd bought a kilo of Silesian brawn in Prague on Na poříčí, and Mr Franc, my neighbour, and I went out at dusk to the Hájenka, it was a Monday, and people drove over from the neighbouring villages, from Hradišťko, and they drank and the pub was packed . . . there was room in the corner, so Mr Franc and I sat down beside two young men I'd never seen before, I sensed they were police assistants, you can tell, but I said, nothing can happen, I'm with Mr Franc, respected citizen of this whole forest area . . . The minute we arrive Mr Franc says: In the name of the Union of Fighters against Fascism, greetings . . . and we sat down, I unwrapped my brawn and offered some to the pair beside me, who refused . . . and I saw, over at the table by the bar, my sister-in-law and dozens of Hradišťko customers beckoning us to come over and sit with them, to leave the place where we were sitting . . . But I said to myself, nothing can happen, let these police assistants see me sit beside them, just like I sit with the local police assistants from Velenka, and Semice . . . But Mr Franc horrified me, calling over to the table which was luring us to change seats, I'm not going to go and sit down with those Communist whores . . . And I was horrified, and in order to recover myself, I ate up practically the whole kilo of Silesian brawn . . . And next morning the Volga came from Nymburk, and first the oral questions, what was going on in the Hájenka? What kind of incident and insults occurred during my presence there? And I didn't recall a thing, nor did Mr Franc, visited by the Volga a minute later . . . A year later I received a summons, as a witness to the fact that Mr Franc had called out: I'm not going to go and sit down with those Communist whores . . . They took my statement at the station in Nymburk, I'd heard it right enough, but Mr Franc is my neighbour and friend, so I claimed I'd heard him say . . . I'm not going to go and sit down with those Communist boys . . . For a while the chief tried to convince me I'd heard what I actually heard, but in the end I signed for Communist boys, because Mr Franc knew all those boys from Sokol gymnastics . . . Then it came to court, and Mr Franc's daughter paced up and down the corridor hissing with anger . . . Something's going to burn today in Kersko! And she spat in front of me . . . then came the court, and the judge insisted I'd heard: I'm not going to go and sit down with those Communist whores, and I insisted I'd heard: I'm not going to go and sit down with those Communist boys . . . so these two sentences played a kind of ping-pong in the chamber, and finally the verdict came that it was indeed Communist whores, but I went on insisting it was boys . . . and so it ended, Mr Franc was fined six hundred crowns, his daughter Věra was waiting in the corridor, and we drove to Kersko in my car, with Věra still going on about how I should've said I didn't hear anything, but I knew they would've taken away my driving licence, because a deaf person isn't allowed to drive . . . because those two we were sitting with in the Hájenka and offering brawn from Silesia were police assistants, they were obliged to say what they'd heard . . . because there were two of them . . . even though the statement of only one police officer constitutes sufficient evidence . . . And Věra stopped speaking to me, and Mr Franc only sort of reluctantly, and I was just submissively, humbly fearful, because it seems to be my fate, to encounter these unpleasant things from time to time . . .

So I can't be at all surprised at what I read in *Literary News*, a piece by my friend from the past, Ivan Klíma. 'The Two Hrabals.' Yes, from his point of view he's quite right, but how did it come about? Let me recall. Once during those years of totalitarianism Irena Zítková, the publishing editor, wanted to get a book out of me. Mr Michálek brought me a collection of photographs of Libeň. And I had the texts of *Too Loud A Solitude* and *The Tender Barbarian* . . . so what did I do? I cut up these texts and put together a new book, a collage to go with the photographs. Then Irena had this text turned down at the Central Committee, by some old gent . . . So I committed an error, albeit *bona fide*, I cut out Jesus Christ, seeing as it bothered the old gent, and Lao Tzu . . . and in fact the result was a new product, Irena as editor was satisfied, the photographer was satisfied, and I was somewhere else — in a state of blame, so now I have to read about this double face of mine, and serve me right!

But my beginnings were altogether strange . . . when I brought Břetislav Chrtek my first text, the book of stories *Lark on a String*, he was delighted, but the publishing house Naše vojsko ('Our Army') couldn't undertake it. So I tried Československý spisovatel ('Czechoslovak Writer') and again, Mr Branald and František Pilař, as private persons, were delighted, but a month later Franta Pilař said to me . . . Look, dear boy, we can't publish this, it'd cost me and Branald our jobs . . . So they gave it back, and I corrected it, cutting out the rude words and dicey situations, and brought it back again . . . but meanwhile things had changed and a certain poet from Samotín had come in as director. And the revised text went to the printers and when the galleys arrived, the poet from Samotín himself, who liked me as a person, but not as a house author, brought them allergically into sales, showed everybody my *Lark on a String* and exclaimed: You want to publish this filth? And he threw away the pages . . . so practically the same text only came out six years later, in 1962 . . . and another director called Pilař — Jan, gave me the publishing house prize for it . . . It's hard publishing books in this country, even back then I started fearing my own texts and I still fear them to this day, though otherwise I just sit around drinking my beer and people say I'm fun to be with . . .

The poet's name was Fikar, he stayed on as director of Československý spisovatel till he became head of the Šmída-Fikar group at the Barrandov film studios . . . that was another totalitarian stroke of fate, for it was with him that Jiří Menzel and I shot our film *Closely Observed Trains*, for which Menzel received not only the Mannheim prize, but even an Oscar . . . But I'm glad to have read Ivan Klíma's piece, he's a man of character, whereas I, as I discover and am afraid to say in essence, am rather a man of no character, because I'm afraid, I have these afterthoughts, *Treppengedanken*, as I leave the court, on the way home I say to myself the things I should've said in there, or I say them over my beer. My wife Pipsi didn't have an easy time of it with me at all. I don't want to flatter myself, but I often used to be not just a right old dreamer, but also a big rogue. What can we do about it . . .

That blond chappy from the tile-clad Ministry meant well by me. He was also a bit of a right old dreamer, always trying to protect me from Vaculík, though one of his colleagues, and he boasted of this, after writing a statement with Vaculík, gave him an apple, as a sign that even though he was a class enemy, he'd gained his sympathies. It also happened one day that an Austrian reporter turned up with a crew, her name was Coudenhove something-or-other, Jewish in appearance. Said she'd do a big show with me along with the others . . . and she brought me a blue bakelite pail full of blue grapes which she'd got near Most where the vine is already growing on the slag heaps . . . And I was scared . . . But no political stuff, *meine liebe Frau, nur nicht jüdische chutzpe*, no Jewish chutzpah . . . heh-heh-heh, I laughed . . . And immediately someone came with a microphone, and I watched my step, as the blond chappy from the tile-clad Ministry had groomed me, and answered only about how my literary work was coming along here in the forest, and how the local air here made me think of the people with whom I live and how I'd never want to live anywhere else . . . I even made the cameraman my guest and saw them all off in front of the gate, and I was happy about how Blondy would be pleased with me this time, how, as Mr Marysko puts it, the wolf had had his fill and the nanny's breast stayed whole . . . A fortnight later the phone rang, with Blondy's voice on the other end, saying, tomorrow at the Belvedere, first floor, it's always empty there, we need to get right down to business . . . and once again I couldn't sleep, even if the waiter in his French piqué from the Belvedere waited to see me at U Sojků, nudged me with his elbow and said . . . look, haven't you caused yourself enough shame as it is? Those cops sit there with you and when we stand in the corner of the bar we can hear every word, for Christ's sake, stick up for yourself a bit, don't get me wrong, but don't shit on yourself like that, those are lousy swine . . . the waiter confided in his French piqué . . . And I couldn't sleep all night, my wife woke up too and called to me, as only she knew how, like someone calling to a crazed horse . . . Whoa-whoa-whoa-whoa-whoa. Well now, tell the cops to go to hell! But I had those genes in me, grandpa's shooting scene from that yard in Židenice, when I was still in the tummy of my mother, whom I never really loved, until she was dying . . . and now I was afraid to look at myself in the mirror, I'd started shaving off at an angle, so as not to see those scared eyes . . . and there on the first floor Blondy kept gripping his briefcase with both hands, he'd brought his bewhiskered pal with him too, I had to autograph my *Poetry Clubs* and some older books as well, and then it started, they gave me the text of the broadcast to read, the one I'd done with Mrs Coudenhove something-or-other for this Austrian free radio station . . . and there I read what these hard boys had with them on the tape . . . Here we are at the centre of Europe, in its very heart . . . The heavy jackboot of Bolshevik power tramples on the throat of an unhappy nation, courageously lamenting beneath the heel of the Soviet boot, and Moscow even has the gall to bend over this subjugated nation and listen to hear if its intellectuals are really choking for breath . . . and then Bohumil Hrabal . . . Life is fine for me living here in the Kersko woods, writing my texts on that freedom which is not only mine but also the freedom of my friends, with whom I drink my beer, in order to escape the pressure of my everyday cares . . . and then once again in German . . . And the Bolshevik jackboot not only tramples on the throat of the Czech nation, it even twists its heel, in order to complete its work of destruction . . . then the former minister Hájek spoke saying, he's happy to be at home, he even takes some nice walks into the fields, in the company of the person acting as his carer, for he still feels not entirely fit after his recent illness . . . and again the commenting voice of Austrian free radio . . . Totalitarianism and its bedfellows celebrate their triumphant success in this land, Mr President Husák may rest content, the nation's freedom is silenced . . . and again my little voice . . . Out here in Kersko it's lovely not only in spring, but especially, like today, in autumn . . . it's the late Indian summer, when the grape ripens, Chinese summer, the thirteenth month, as I read in Bruno Schulz's *The Cinnamon Shops* . . . Enough, said Blondy, now you can hear and see for yourself, Mr Hrabal, we gave you plenty of warning, now you hear how you've been misused, not only you, but one of Dubček's former ministers . . . What can we do? I asked, and suddenly I felt really scared that this Mrs Coudenhove what-d'you-call-it . . . had pulled a fast one on me . . . Well, said Blondy, that's up to you, you've been drawn into our game . . . write a letter expressing your outrage, saying you've been misused by this Austrian journalist by a speech and a . . . what do you call it, said Blondy. I said: A collage . . . right, a collage, say you protest and we'll send this letter to the Austrian Ambassador in person . . . and the trio from the Interior Ministry sat round me so I formed the centre of their equilateral triangle . . . while there at the back the waiter stood in semi-darkness, his French piqué gleaming with whiteness, but his eyes, even as his fingers wrapped cutlery in napkins, were furious, no longer with the cops, but with me . . . and the blood rushed to my temples, eyes and cheeks, I flushed with false and unseemly shame . . . And so I wrote this letter to the Austrian Ambassador in Prague, I even did feel a little that the Coudenhove woman had deceived me, that she hadn't kept her promise . . . And then with Blondy I posted the letter registered mail from the same post-office as the letter to Vaculík and Ivan Havel three months before . . . And it was a bombshell . . . the Ambassador, his name was the same as the President of Austria's, sent me a letter, I've got it somewhere . . . but the main point was, he told me off politely, saying Austria was a free country, with freedom of the press, their journalists enjoyed freedom, and if I liked I could sue Mrs Coudenhove whatever-her-name for what was on the radio, but not complain to the Austrian Ambassador, it was the first time it had ever happened to him, he said, and he was particularly surprised after the information he'd had about me that I was an independent writer, well-known not just in Europe, but in Austria as well, which means something . . . and again the telephone rang and I said . . . Yes, I know, the answer's come, I'll bring it along, but let's meet on the path by the Brussels Pavilion, where the kids go to play, it's nice today, maybe it'll be nice tomorrow too, I said . . . And off I went for another beer, to drink one after another and so forget about everything happening to literature in this country at present . . . It dawned on me that our literature, official literature, was really being run by the Ministry of the Interior, they wanted to train me up to be just such another writer as Ivan Skála or Jan Pilař, like the young generation of poets and fiction writers . . . And so I, born in the year nineteen-fourteen under the old Austria, and nursed on Austrian milk, had written something abhorrent to that little Austrian land of mine, I'd slandered the Café Hawelka and the Hotel zur Post in Albach, where I'd imbibed my Innsbruck ten-degree beer and my Obstler Liqueur . . . horror, I was scared to think of what I'd perpetrated thanks to my weakening and allowing myself to be drawn into the caring hands of the Ministry of the Interior . . . it was a disease, I couldn't exist without the anticipation of that call from Blondy asking to speak to me on an urgent matter . . .

Two pals of mine from the Hájenka were assistants of the police. Franta Vorel, I used to go to his pig slaughterings, and if I didn't have time, he'd bring me out to the hacienda a can of soup from the sausage making and black puddings and sausages, later brawn as well. Franta brought a lot of fun to the Hájenka! When he'd had a few, he danced on the table, or on the large Fiľakovo stove, he was friends with all the customers, even though everyone knew he was a police assistant . . . The second fellow was called the White Gypsy . . . he was silvery grey haired, had a damaged nose, knew about wild mushrooms, where they grew and when, and he used to sit in the Hájenka, apparently paying no attention to the conversations, but listening and smoking, and he called me Bohouš . . . That was the way of it here, same as in the Prague pubs where I went drinking, you didn't distinguish who was who, we were even surprised to discover, maybe ten years later, that so-and-so was in the Party, of whom we'd never have thought it . . . The White Gypsy used to direct our May Day parades, he stood at the outskirts of Semice stopping the cars with his raised lollipop until the May Day parade was over . . . And I used to join the procession every year, it went from one end of the village to the other, passing itself doubled up several times over, and we greeted and waved at each other all over again, each time we passed, as if we were seeing each other for the first time . . . These processions were more or less analogous to the Corpus Christi parades in Nymburk I used to take part in . . . And there was a platform in front of the council building, district party people spoke and young pioneers solemnly promised, and a speaker always came from Milovice . . . On one occasion the White Gypsy rebuked me gently for having a pee behind the bus shelter on the village green, just when the delegate from Milovice was speaking, headmistress of the local school . . .

And at the time of my public scandal, after I got back home, two bearded young men turned up, and one of them introduced himself as Kadlec . . . he pulled a bundle of samizdats out of his bag and said there were thirty of them, I was to keep one and autograph the rest . . . It was *Vacant Lots* . . . which I was afraid of not only when I was writing it, but also when Jarda Kladiva and I had it copied by that ministry lady on fine paper . . . But now it was a typical samizdat . . . And I trembled with fear, I knew at once that by now one of the copies would be in the hands of Blondy at the Ministry, and he'd call me when the time came . . . So I autographed those twenty-nine *Vacant Lots*, my hand shook, but I signed . . . Škvorecký had published it already, and I, who had walked this morning in the May Day parade and exchanged waves with the passing participants, this afternoon signed my name on these samizdat *Vacant Lots* . . . And you know, that Interior Ministry philosopher, who visited me once a month and impressed it upon me that our literature had to go with the people, he taught me in the end to write quickly, at one fell swoop, à la prima, that's actually how I wrote those nine hundred pages, called *Weddings in the House*, and the third part is *Vacant Lots*, which frightened me the most . . . In the end the Interior Ministry, having taken on the advisory role of Czechoslovak Writer, finally forced me to make use of my fear, go on fearing, but also go on writing, because the only defence against fear in the end was this literature, this typewriter of mine . . .

And Mr Kadlec and I met up in Prague, he worked somewhere on cybernetic duplicating machines, we sat in the Formanka on Veletržní, opposite Paliárka . . . and I agreed to Mr Kadlec's offer, that we'd start publishing everything I'd written and never published, because I've no idea really how *Vacant Lots* found its way to Canada to Mr Škvorecký and his wife . . . And so later I was sitting in the Plzeňský dvůr, when Blondy came in, clutching his briefcase to him, he was pale and without uttering a word he threw *Vacant Lots* on the table, one of those I'd been signing in Kersko on that afternoon of the First of May . . . And before he went away, Blondy arranged that we'd meet the next day at the Belvedere, in front of the entrance . . . And I sat over my beer, *Vacant Lots* lay there in front of me, I was neither in time nor in space, but in the very heart of horror and dread and that fear of mine which I'd inherited in my genes . . . and the beauty of it was, I couldn't even stand, I was paralysed for a while, I knew that once Škvorecký had published my *Vacant Lots*, they'd publish it anywhere else they got it to read . . . it'd be published not only in Canada, not only in America, but in Europe too . . . and because with this Ministry education I'd risen over and above myself, I didn't care any more, I wished only to die . . . And then I got up after all, with my feet dragging, I paid and rushed off to the Formanka, Mr Kadlec could see from a distance how scared I was, and I told him I was cancelling our agreement, I'd just been sitting with a secret police-man, who'd brought me *Vacant Lots* and they'd be wanting to know where it was printed and by whom . . .

And so it was, Blondy asked me on the first floor of the Belvedere . . . but he wasn't officious, he was affable even, he only wanted to know who had given me those *Vacant Lots*, because like an idiot I'd gone and revealed that a young man had come and handed me thirty copies . . . and I was so weakened that I said I didn't know where the young man lived, but his name was Karafiát . . .

By that time I was afraid to stay in at my Kersko hacienda. I liked to walk down Farská cesta to the fields, where there was a stack of straw, and there I dug myself in and watched the hares and pheasants come along, I was safe from those dozens of journalists and photographers descending upon me, that doctor of philoso-phy wouldn't track me down here, he who actually made me write, by shouting at me . . . So it's either Vaculík, or you and your wife can go to the sea at Salonika . . . and so, during the fine weather I was dug into the straw, it was warm here, though it was only the end of May . . . And there I was, taking my ease, when suddenly along Farská cesta I saw the Volga coming, it stopped, and the Sadská chief jumped out, hair oiled and in his best uniform, Vlasta his name was, and he walked over to me, signalling to me not to worry . . . he had a pair of binoculars on his chest and I was so hor-rified I couldn't stand up, it was just as well I was buried in that straw up to my neck . . . and Vlasta — you see, the horror of it makes me forget his surname even, though we sat together often in the Hájenka . . . Vlasta swept aside the straw, lay down beside me and took something out of his official bag . . . I half-closed my eyes, thinking he'd pull out a copy of *Vacant Lots*, but he only took out his notebook . . . we lay there and he confessed to me he'd like to write, was it difficult to become a writer? And so, just as the Interior Ministry officials had indirectly taught me how to write without prejudice, from the heart straight on to the typewriter, now I was supposed to teach the Sadská police chief how to write . . . I conducted this course five times in all, he drove up in the Volga and lay down beside me . . . I brought him Babel's *Red Cavalry*, but he gave it back saying he'd never manage it, so I gave him early Chekhov short stories and he liked that . . . But finally I got an idea . . . Look, chief, write your stories the way you'd write a report, about the lads from Mans, from Chrást, maybe the one about how they pulled the transmitter cables off the Volga and chased the policemen round the field and thrashed them with those wires until reinforcements arrived and the police won, how they gave the lads from Mans a good thumping and put the bracelets on them, handcuffs, and took them to the nick . . .

And I used to ride the bus out from Prague to Kersko, I felt calm in the bus, what Interior Ministry official would take the bus with me to Kersko? But one day . . . There at the bus-station stood Blondy, clutching his briefcase in both hands, waiting beneath the number 18 bus sign, and there was still time, a quarter of an hour before departure . . . we sat down on a bench and Blondy took out a file, a pile of index cards with a photograph of a man on each, and a text, and Blondy asked me to look carefully through them, and if any of them looked like Karafiát, I was to tell him . . . the bus by now was ready for departure and we were still in the middle of searching for Karafiát's face . . . I sighed with relief that I had to get on the bus, but Blondy got on with me, so we sat right at the back, on the last seats, and Karafiát wasn't anywhere to be found . . . Blondy only got off at the bend near Mochov, he advertised me to the driver, because he had him stop by showing his ID, there was no bus-stop . . . and by now I was totally flummoxed . . . I mean, I used to sit around with Karafiát in pubs, Blondy or his friends could've identified and checked him over when we were sitting there with our beers, but over in the Ministry they were really glad they could fill me with horror and I wasn't able to say what Iago said after the murders . . . And from this moment on my lips are dumb . . . What might they do to me?

And so it came about, that my friends and Mr Kadlec's friends started calling him Mr Karafiát . . . and my brother, who used to sit in the Hájenka and chat away neatly to the police assistants, told me one day that the White Gypsy had a confidential message for me, it was a very important matter, he needed to speak to me . . . so I went to the Hájenka, it was afternoon, the White Gypsy was sitting as always right by the door, stroking his silvery grey hair, just like I once did, combing the remnants of hair across from ear to ear, he shone with hair-oil, smoked and was all solemn, drank coffee and we chatted for a bit about football, Semice had won and Mikluščák, my footballer of the year, had covered himself with glory . . . and then there was silence, and the White Gypsy whispered to me . . . Look, an official from the Interior Ministry came to see me, invited me over to the Husarka in Sadská, he had some papers with him, and I was surprised . . . Bohouška, this is for your ears only . . . this guy in the Husarka told me you write books which people publish abroad . . . but they haven't got them at the Ministry, and he asked me, seeing as we're pals like, to tell you, that they'd like to read those books too . . . That's what the White Gypsy whispered in my ear, and his lips were cold, and I remembered how one day Blondy and I conducted our hearing on the path above the Brussels pavilion and he too whispered . . . The lads from the Ministry want me to say they'd also like to read those books of yours . . . And now I was sitting in the Hájenka with the White Gypsy, he laid his hand on the back of mine, and I drew back, then leaned over again, so he wouldn't take umbrage, and I coughed and said . . . But I've given them all away, I don't have them any more . . . And I looked in his eyes, I saw his terrible nose, ridden with some disease, he'd taken retirement with shortened veins in both arms, so that his fingers were numb, they were clenched . . . and he ordered vodkas — Bohoušku, let's drink to our health, I've not got much of it left . . . and when we'd downed the glasses, he bent over once more and whispered . . . I've got cancer, I know it . . . but I'd still like to read that *Vacant Lots* . . . I took fright: What *Vacant Lots*? . . . Vlasta, the chief . . . he's got it already . . .

Journalists kept on coming, visiting Kersko and my flat and my pubs, and they heightened my fear . . . I spotted them the moment they entered, I knew they'd want to film me and have me give them accounts of my thoughts, my work and so on . . . and I went crazy, I started to get abusive . . . But one day a journalist came from Germany and said he and his crew only wanted to do a kind of scene taken from life, from the pub . . . and I said tomorrow was Saturday and U kocoura was having a get-together of its old masters, the

Kocours, the pub was set aside from ten in the morning till three in the afternoon, and I was getting a diploma, that would be something for the TV, and lovely singing you get there, in short the golden days of old with top-notch food and drink, finishing up with a group photo of the Kocours outside this Malá Strana alehouse . . . So we fixed it for the Saturday, and I asked them to clear it with the manager, tell him what this West German TV lot wanted to do . . . And I went to Kersko on the Friday, sat with my beer, the pub was full, night had fallen . . . and who comes up the steps out of the dark into the light, but Blondy. He came in, looking for me, searching through practically all the faces before he found mine . . . and we went out and he asked me, pleaded and begged me, to call off the filming at U kocoura, to cancel it in my own interest . . . and he gave me the telephone number for the film crew, and asked me to call them up, saying the producer would make a compromising scene not only for me, but also for the Kocours, of whom a third were Communists . . . so I dialed the number in the kitchen, and strangely enough the same man answered with whom I had arranged this great handing out of prizes and diplomas and birthday jubilees, and I told him I was calling it off . . . And he said he was only production, his TV boss was out somewhere meeting Vaculík, he'd give him the message, that I, Bohumil Hrabal, didn't want any filming to take place at U kocoura . . . And Blondy thanked me, and I thanked him too, for now everyone in the pub knew I'd been talking in the Hájenka with the secret police on a surely important matter . . .

And early next morning, as I was feeding the cats, a Mercedes drove up and out stepped the producer with whom I'd arranged that show with the old Kocours at U kocoura, and once again and over again I had to repeat, that I didn't want to take part in this filming, obstinately he asked me whether I really meant it . . . and I did . . . I stared at the ground, I went red, but I insisted I meant it . . . But I never said who Karafiát was.

So I sat in the Tiger sunk in deep thought, this loud solitude was getting to me, now I remembered that the chap I taught how to write in the stack of straw by Farská cesta with its view out over the countryside past Velenka church to Paleček, Mr Hamáček's old field, that police chief's name was Vlasta Ulrich . . . in the end he shot himself with his duty pistol in the cellar of his Sadská police office . . . I remembered that the last time I saw Blondy was when the Interior Ministry had now decided to leave me alone . . . Just as I entered the foreign section of the Writers' Union to get my passport to the USA, I bumped into him in the doorway to the manageress's office, we blocked the entrance, and he, clutching that briefcase of his with both hands, went red, and I said, what are you doing here? And he mumbled . . . issuing passports for writers . . . But Mr Hrabal! We knew who Karafiát was from the very start . . .

So here I sat in the Tiger with Motýlek, I was quiet for over two hours, and he likes that too, customers came and went, but Motýlek signalled to them with a raised hand that they should leave me alone . . . And I returned to reality and said . . . Motýlek, is there any *Večerní Praha*, do you have an Expres?

I was quiet for over two hours, telling myself instead of the Danish lady about those images that frighten me over and over again . . . The White Gypsy died a couple of weeks after we drank

those two Russian vodkas together . . . so fulfilling the sentence I
didn't believe . . . Bohouši, won't you drink to my health, as I'm
dying?

Motýlek took in a breath beside me, his huge chest stretching
his Italian sweater . . . my friend Motýlek, who did nine years in
Leopoldov for accidentally killing a policeman as a young man . . .
he took in a breath and declared: I'm going to act as a bodyguard
for you, Mr Hrabal . . . like President Havel has.

P.S.

In the end I discover it's all in the genes . . . I'm told this by
Professor Štork, every week he gets a special magazine for hospital consultants from the USA, and there it says that in the end
everything in a person, his physical and mental destiny, is just as
the Fates decree before birth, doubly so at the birth itself . . . and
so one person gets a tall candle, another a middle-sized one and a
third only a tiny little candle . . . and the one with the tall candle
can drink and smoke and live to be eighty, unless he's carried off
by unnatural causes . . . and the one that gets the tiny little candle,
maybe doesn't smoke and doesn't drink and watches his diet and
so on, still goes under the sod at the age of thirty . . .

And this nation, do what it may, has Master Jan Hus in its
genes, and the Reformation, even as Roman Catholics . . . My rela-
tion Baron Lánský z Růže, Mr Kocián, told me that his uncle was
in Vienna, in a Dominican monastery, he was the prior, and only
his mother could visit him . . . and the mother looked in a bedside
table drawer in the rooms of this Dominican son of hers, and there
was a portrait of Jan Hus . . . And my relatives told me, when some

people railed at me for being a drunkard, my female cousin stood up for me, saying that on my granddad's side, my great-grandfather used to be so drunk that he never got home, he ended up lying in the ditch, till his grown-up sons, rather than have their dad be like that, beat him up so badly where he lay, that after that he only drank just enough that he was still able to stagger back home . . . I've got this drinking in my genes, and there's nothing to be done with it, just like this nation . . . not all, but most of the population has in its genes an inclination for Bolsheviks, Communists, Marxists, because, Dubenka, when voting was secret in the First Republic, behind a screen, the Communists got something over a million votes . . . As I've written to you, for almost a whole year I was, not just a Party member, but district secretary in Nymburk for cultural affairs. And that was enough for me for the rest of my life. I left with a postcard saying that the same reasons which had led me into the Party now led me out of it, I asked them from the sixteenth of June 1946 no longer to register me as a Communist Party member, to strike my name off the list . . . So this nation has in its genes what I have in mine . . . an inclination for booze and for Communism . . .

Written in Kersko, 9th-11th November 1990

The Rosenkavalier

Miss April,

A few days ago, on the 28th April, David Černý, student of sculpture at the Prague School of Applied Arts, went over to Smíchov, to the Square of the Soviet Tank-Corps, and painted its green memorial tank a rosy pink. For, as he said to the journalists, pink is the colour of a babe in arms, a symbol of innocence . . . All day long onlookers flocked to see this unreal thing which had actually come to pass . . . Cameramen rushed, while there was yet time, to film this wondrous sight of Prague, which knocked Allan Kaprow's one-time happenings into a cocked hat . . . And it was some time before the army came to drape a green military tarpaulin over this pink tank . . . Policemen went into the School of Applied Art, infringing sovereign academic soil, and all day long they subjected one female student to forensic examination, all because she wore pink boots . . . as Martin Šmíd reported in the Metropolitan . . . Later on the soldiers painted the pink tank green again . . . The things that go on here in Prague . . . I was only sorry they demolished Stalin's monument all those years ago . . . Can you imagine, Miss April, what a wondrous sight that would've been, if David Černý had used his pink paint on Stalin as well? . . . In one fell swoop this would've made Prague the world centre for pop-art, a happening like this here in Prague would've set the crown on that

American school initiated those years ago by Allan Kaprow, Claes Oldenburg and the rest . . . not forgetting our own Milan Knížák or Eugene Brikcius . . .

Miss April, on this last day of April Prague was on the march again, just like in the November Hurricane of '89. Hundreds of thousands of people, young, old and lame, all rushing to feast the Burning of the Witches, according to the ancient Slav custom, inherited from the Celts, of celebrating the last day of April with drinking and orgies.

And I, in my "girl's" pink scarf, struggled to the bank, to get me some Deutschmarks to purchase this video from Charlie, which features me as well as the rest of his wedding. I got hooked on the idea of having this video, because, says I, what if I were to die? What a splendid thing it would be to be seen going about at this wedding with a boa constrictor round my neck, adding to that myth of myself as a bit of a lad about town. You see, April, the wedding in question happened last year, I saw the video at the time, and I'd almost forgotten its existence, yet there I was in it, a treasure going to waste. What a wedding it was too! The bride was stunning in her wedding dress of Valenciennes lace, with a rose in her hair, the music was semi-Gypsy, the groom was in a DJ, smoking a cigar, with his hair in a parting, and the guests sat about drinking and eating, or wandered about from table to table, while I, Miss April, sat by the window, when all of a sudden something touched my ear . . . it did it again . . . And the guests opposite looked on with bulging eyes, staring at what I too soon found myself face to face with . . . I swung about, and there right opposite me was the head of a snake flicking its red tongue at my ear, over my shoulder and round my neck, and once more this beautiful great snake went and wound itself right around me, it was rosy pink and gold, gleaming like a head of corn on the cob . . . And it gazed lovingly into my eyes, so what could I do? It was my fate . . . my destiny . . . I stood up, and that snake was really heavy . . . A certain lady there, one of Charlie's guests, told me it was hers, that snake, it was a strangler, the last time it had strangled and eaten was only the day before yesterday, a boa constrictor it was, but she would keep a good eye on me, so that nothing would go wrong, the groom had refused to have it round his neck . . . So I walked about the place wearing this snake, and the wedding guests were scared, some were jealous, and at last I became what in fact I am, a bit of an old comedian, a bit of a ham, for, you see, art, Miss April, involves a certain amount of hamming it up, a certain amount of the old Schmieren-komediantentum, as Friedrich Nietzsche put it, writing on *Why I write such beautiful books* . . .

Miss April, tell Dubenka I even took the snake over to the table beneath the Great Antlers where the bride was sitting, she'd just finished sharing a plate of dumpling soup with the groom . . . I sat myself down beside her, her dress of Valenciennes lace glistened like the skin of the pink boa constrictor, I sat beside the bride, who leaned her head over, and the snake's red tongue whispered words of love in her ear . . . The table was redolent with bunches of roses, and the snake clasped me so tight that I went slightly red, and just for a moment I had the distinct tactile sense that this boa was Dubenka, code for my attachment to her, a long arm extending all the way from San Francisco over to Prague . . . So I stood up again, and I walked through the festivities, the music moved along, now in front of me, now behind, bow-strings and Gypsy eyes accompanied me, and I saw that nobody else would've dared to do what I did, for this snake was a strangler, it weighed six kilograms, it was cold, as though made of brass, it smelt just a little of musk and rosy perfume . . . And it would only have had to wind itself a little bit more round my neck, and the coil would have strangled me . . . Moreover I acquiesced in this, for I had the tactile sense that this snake was Dubenka, and I said — If I had to choose how to die . . . then this would be the right death, to be strangled by this boa constrictor . . . That's what I said, but its owner took fright, she said . . . If Sisa starts squeezing you any tighter than this, you've got to stick the fingers of both hands under its tightening grip, otherwise I'll have to run and get a knife from the kitchen . . . Look, I'm really getting a bit nervous about this, she said . . . But I was just on top of the world, Miss April, I loved it, even though I could feel the boa gripping my neck and its little red tongue flickering ominously about . . . I saw its owner fling open the door to the kitchen — but then she went out the other door into the passage, with its steps leading up to the first floor where she was staying . . . I could see the illumined stairs rising, first of all her head appeared, then her ascending body, then the her body disappeared, I only saw her knees and white stockings, till they vanished too, and only her shoes could be seen as she pattered up the stairs . . . Then she was totally gone, only her footsteps could be heard upstairs . . . Shortly after that she came back down, leading by the hand a lovely little girl in a pink dress . . . She came into the bar with this little girl, who was beautiful, just like Deanna Durbin in the film *One Hundred Men and a Girl* . . . The little girl bowed, bobbed a little curtsy, then she proffered her elbow, and the boa constrictor slowly unwound itself from my neck, and slowly it slid across my elbow on to the girl's shoulders . . . And now the little lassie carried the snake through the bar, again my boa constrictor was the centre of attention, while I turned pale, Sisa's owner wiped the perspiration off me with a hankie, and I smiled. I could only just manage to sit down beside the bride, I touched her hip, my hand was shaking, and her dress of Valenciennes lace was cold. Charlie came over with a glass of champagne, so we drank to my having made myself an adornment of his feast . . .

Miss April, so I've told you the story of what I expect my friends and I will see again on the video I bought from Charlie, I'm curious to see if I'll be as touched by it as I was six months ago at Charlie's wedding, a thousand marks I shelled out for that magnificent video, because I had this vision of me dying soon, and the video would become the property of Prague Imagination, my publishers . . . what a fine thing that'll be, when I die, and Prague Imagination sell the video clips all over the world, earning money for Mr Karafiát to print new writers' debuts in rosy pink jackets . . . pink, like the "girl's" scarf I bought in Strasbourg . . . My friend and translator Sergio Corduas, whenever he came to Prague, always without fail he wore a pink scarf . . . and just as they used to ask him, so people in the Golden Tiger ask me, why I wear this girl's scarf . . .

Miss April, then the day came for the screening of the video . . . and it was defective, with a kind of snowflakes falling all the time down the videotape, as if the Golden Tiger's ceiling had gone and rain was showering down diagonally over the wedding . . . But the main point of it was still there, what really mattered, it achieved what I had in mind, a kind of death insurance, so that ultimately these video clips of me, no more than ten minutes in all, could one day be seen across all the screens of the world, making me number one, for wearing this boa constrictor at the Golden Tiger . . . But above all — since Prague is Golden Prague, where all kinds of weird and wonderful things happen — just so that Dubenka can be proud I'm not really such a wet rag as I like to make out in my letters . . .

Miss April, pass on the message to Dubenka that I'm starting to go soft in the head, tell her, when we showed this video of Charlie's wedding, I ended up agreeing with the words of Tomáš Mazal, that in view of what happened to that old girl of a tank, maybe the height of achievement would be just to wipe the video clean so that only the empty tape remained, with one great pink Nothingness on it, price a thousand marks . . . the Nothingness contemplated by Heidegger and the ancient Indian philosophers . . . Tell Dubenka also, that here in Prague we were captivated by that young German who, at the age of seventeen, on Soviet Air Force Day, crept in wolf-like with his aeroplane through guarded air-space all the way from Sweden to the Kremlin in Moscow, the traffic policeman even guided him in, to stop him hitting the overhead wires, he just glided over the bridge and straight into Red Square, bobbing up lightly against the Kremlin wall — and two women, carrying bunches of roses, going to pay homage to Lenin, gave their bouquets to the pilot instead . . . Just as similarly we were captivated these last few days by David Černý, who, using false papers, right before the eyes of the police, merrily painted the green Soviet tank pink . . . Miss April, tell Dubenka again that I, so often to be seen in my pink scarf, walked through Charlie's party at the Golden Tiger with a boa constrictor round my neck, enchanting all the wedding guests . . . Mind you now! that boa constrictor wrapped around me like a pink scarf, that was nothing, but those two young men, one in Moscow, and now another in Prague, they have set the crown on our rosy velvet epoch, laid the foundation for a new era, in which they may reign over the world's future . . . Join the Society for the Restoration of the Pink Tank, as Martin Šmíd said in the Metropolitan . . .

P.S.

Miss April, it's the First of May, I'm out in Kersko, it's raining, the whole countryside around is permeated with the scent of blossoming trees and bird cherry, I walk up and down the white fence, breathing in that scent, with my band of cats following after me, last of all comes quietly, timidly my old wet rag of a Cassius, a kind of little villein of his own emigration, he's always last, solitude has polished off the bravery and impudence I once loved in him so much . . . It's raining, it's getting dark, the countryside is quiet, dominated by dark green and blue, broken only by the white glow of my fence and garden gate . . . I'm standing by the fence, beside me rises a great bird cherry tree, its blossoms are white, the breeze ripples through the top of this tree, whose trunk stands there firmly like a great bride, that bird cherry tree shifts like a film projection screen, like a great curtain of Valenciennes lace . . . The band of cats sits round me in a half-circle, all absorbed in their own thing, what I'm doing now, all those girlish feline friends of mine do it, all my little children . . . they're gazing at the flowering bird cherry, sniffing that pungent scent . . . and there . . . last of all sits my Cassius, gazing at the same thing as me . . . all of us captives to Seryozha Yesenin, who also loved so much — to listen intently to the song of the bird cherry trees and the rain . . .

Miss April, I send, by the scent of all the bird cherry trees in the world . . . greetings to Dubenka.

Kersko, May Day rain and föhn [1991]

Translator's Note

These texts, prefaced by 'The Magic Flute', form part of the longer series of *Dopisy Dubence* (Letters to Dubenka), now in volume 13 of the author's collected works (Prague: Pražská imaginace, 1995). The pieces were previously issued in the volumes *Listopadový uragán* (November Hurricane; 1990), *Ponorné říčky* (Subterranean Streams; 1991) and *Růžový kavalír* (The Rosenkavalier; 1991). I also consulted *Kouzelná flétna* (The Magic Flute; 1990), and some original versions published in the press or as individual pamphlets.

The choice of texts is my own. Three versions were previously issued as follows: 'Meshuge Stunde' in *Storm*, no. 1 (1991), edited by Joanna Labon; 'The White Horse' in *Cape*, no. 2 (1992), edited by Nicholas Pearson; 'The Rosenkavalier' (as 'The Pink Scarf') in the Picador anthology *Description of a Struggle*, edited by Michael March (London, 1994). I am indebted to my three previous editors, and Howard Sidenberg of Twisted Spoon Press, for their help, encouragement and useful suggestions.

Oxford, September 1997

BOHUMIL HRABAL was born in 1914 in the Moravian town of Brno-Židenice, but spent his childhood in Nymburk, a town that forms the backdrop for many of his stories. He came to Prague in the late 1930s to study at the Law School of Charles University, where he received his degree. After the war he settled permanently in Prague and began to write on a regular basis. An initial flirtation with Surrealism gave way to what he called "total realism" in his writing, which was a reflection of the time he spent working at the Kladno ironworks in the 1950s. Over the subsequent decades he held many jobs while continuing to write a great number of stories and novels. Considered a major stylistic innovator, Hrabal introduced the "palaverer" into Czech fiction. Many contemporary European writers now point to him as a major influence, and he was awarded some of the top literary honors at home and abroad. Among his most renowned works are *Closely Watched Trains*, *I Served the King of England*, and *Too Loud A Solitude*. He died in 1997 after falling from his hospital window while trying to feed the pigeons.

JAMES NAUGHTON is Professor of Czech Language and Literature at Oxford University. He is the translator of *The Little Town Where Time Stood Still* by Bohumil Hrabal and *The Jingle Bell Principle* by Miroslav Holub.

TOTAL FEARS by Bohumil Hrabal / translated from the Czech
by James Naughton / monotype on cover by Vladimír Boudník /
frontispiece photo by Tomáš Mazal / design by Chaim / text set in
Janson / published by Twisted Spoon Press: P.O. Box 21—Preslova
12, 150 21 Prague 5, Czech Republic, www.twistedspoon.com /
printed in the Czech Republic / distributed in North America by SCB
DISTRIBUTORS: 15608 South New Century Drive, Gardena, CA
90248, info@scbdistributors.com; www.scbdistributors.com

10 9 8 7 6 5 4 3